Children of the Universe

Poetry to Elevate the Reader to the 5th Dimension

When we feed our passions with intention they grow wings of their own and become Children of the Universe

by

Jen Ward

ISBN-13: 978-1530767236
ISBN-10: 1530767237

1st Edition: 2016-04-03
2nd Edition: 2016-11-30
3rd Edition: 2018-09-14

Acknowledgment to Trees

Thank you for all the love and support all the trees in my life have given me. You have nurtured me when no human would; you have felt compassion for me when I was lonely. You admonished me for cutting you down in your prime and taught me a great lesson. You have more passion, wisdom, insights, and awareness than any person I have ever known. Sometimes when I was praying to God, a tree answered.

Trees have been secretly inspiring humans to scribe their words throughout history. A poem in history stated a poem was as lovely as a tree was written by a tree but had a human scribe. Many people who like what I write may be surprised to know that for much of what I write, I am a scribe of the trees. I am honored to collect the wisdom of the trees and share it with others.

In these pages, please enjoy the symbiotic relationship between human and tree. Enjoy the expansiveness of what you are capable of tapping into through what is written. Let it change your vantage point with the world and allow your anchors that define you to fall away. Use this book as a portal into a more amazing relationship with the universe and yourself. You are the reason the trees and I wrote this book.

Discover your own connection with the Divine and all the living beings that it moves through. May you release the fluidity, wisdom, and expansiveness in yourself to live in constant wonderment as well.

Children of the Universe

Table of Contents

Children of the Universe

Introduction

I Once Was a Grape

When I was a teenager, I used to write poetry all the time. I had a little shelf in my room that I used as an altar. It was a combination of rosary, candles, and statues that conjured up something meaningful in me. Poetry would just pour out of me. I felt like I was an altar in the world for others. It was dramatic and driven by the desire for love and God. I remember writing a whole series of poems from the vantage point of a grape that became aware it was part of a bunch of grapes, a vineyard, and eventually wine. It was called, "I Once Was a Grape." It depicts the interconnectedness that I see humanity moving towards.

One day my mother, who took very little interest in me and knew very few people, had a bitter friend who just happened to know someone who worked at the local writers and book club. He was a student with an analytical mind but seemed like an authority to me. She took my poems to him to see if I had any talent. His critique was brutal. He did not take into account the passion or the depth and merely focused on syntax and the rules of proper writing. He barely considered my obvious sensitivities either.

The critique was another reason to go numb inside, except at a deeper level. I had felt this way often with external events but nothing that was so personal. It was like someone had introduced numbing agent to my soul. I stopped writing then. It was a shame. It was such a good coping method.

1

The urge to pour out words in artful dance would emerge once in a while. But it wasn't until life had stripped me down to the bone and taken away all outer distractions like family and friends that writing reemerged as a joy. How else does one express such deep connection to love, joy, wisdom, and truth in the universe? My passion for expression has reemerged.

But it is funny. My writing is not shared to be validated as a writer or wise sage. It is shared to give voice, heart, and reason to all those out there who are smoldering in their passion and need encouragement to burst into empowerment. This book is dedicated to all the seekers, knowers, believers, dreamers, forsaken, discouraged, dismissed, and bewildered. Here is to finding your voice, your truth, or your passion. Here is to needing no one to give you permission to thrive. This book and others that I write are staking claim into the universe and providing safe passage for all others to explore.

Section I: Discovery

Your Dreams

Don't be afraid to dirty the knees
Or get gravel embedded in the palm of each hand
When scaling beyond the highest limitation
Leap into the greater you
Walk across the bridge between wonder and belief
Stand in absolute knowing
That the gnawing ache that churns the stomach with grout
Beats back the spewing lies of fear
That mocks
Of the danger of adopting a new found freedom.
Each leap between belief and realized
Is jumping beyond the pay scale of convention
Your dreams are the expansion of the bigger stroke you use
When actualizing the brush of your own potential.
Let the butterflies free
Give them girth
The bigger your attempts
The wider their wing span
The grandest intentions
Risk the greatest drop into the abyss
Yet the gap is necessary for your own awakening
Every try strengthens the muscles of conviction
Every failure is a success
The real danger is lying curled up in indifference
With the curtains closed to your own potential.

Love's Hue

Stretch your arms into the sky and pluck out the farthest star,
Display it on your bedpost to remember who you are.

Dig with your mind into the earth and find the deepest root,
Remind yourself often of where you come and mark it with your boot.

Delve into the pain you hide from the world and shelter with your tears,
Disarm the things that keep you from knowing that this world is a house of mirrors.

Question all matters, everything that you've ever learned ever since your birth,
Discard all the lies that you readily accepted that prevent you from knowing your worth.

Reawaken the aspect of your sweet self that knows you as being the best,
Forget all the memories that kept you enslaved...they were merely a spiritual test.

You are the Light rooted in earth...the rest is the house of illusion,
Shatter the mirrors, stop believing the lies, let go of the pain and confusion.

Reclaim your spirit! Realize your worth! You were merely asleep...so awaken,

Emanate Joy. Realize Love. Remember that dream you've forsaken.

You are abundance. So cash yourself in. You are the gain that you seek,

A course of miracles in your own book of life, just open you up, take a peek.

You are a windfall. You are your own church. You are a prayer. So just "say you",

A brush stroke of truth swept across the night sky...Loves colorful well blended hue.

2/5/15

Loving by Default

Strip away the angst and fear

Wipe away the grime

Being less than kind to yourself

Is no 2nd degree of crime

Putting others first

Is a noble kind of trait

But doing so as you suffer

Seems loving, but it ain't

Martyring yourself
Piling upon the grief
Is not such a noble cause
That's a limiting belief

True friends want to see you well
It's hard to rely upon the rest
To reflect back the love you give so freely
And wish you all the best

Allow others to receive from you
But don't let them pull you down
You are not a scapegoat,
Puppet or a clown

Give to everyone freely
Just so it's not a self-assault
By loving You as much as others
You are being loving by default.
9/2/15

May All Blessings Be

Any arms are my arms
That reach out to hug
Whether they belong to a saint
Or are attached to a thug

Any pain is my pain
It all cuts so deep
I feel internal angst
Am compelled just to weep

Any life is a value
So worth taking up space
The divine act of existing
It's a contract in Grace

Every Soul is a vantage point
So worth the knowing
By exploring its depth
Enacts our own growing

Any heart is a heart
Well worth the beating
It's better to engage
Than to set out defeating

Every life is valuable
Especially yours
Enlightening yourself
Is like opening doors

You are a valued, respected
Being of pure light
Recognizing your empowerment
Brings the world new delight

What you choose to do
With this expression of you
Impinges the whole world
In what we go through

The more you embrace your greatness
With kindness and Grace
The more this world becomes
An enlightened place

In fact, the whole world
Is a reflection of you
So for the sake of all
Love what you do

Stand by what you say
The truth you command
The fate of the world
Sits in your hand

When you emanate with love
Wherever you go
You are feeding the love
To all those you know

So for the Grace of everyone
The collective "we"
May you be a blessing to all
And May all blessings Be

9/10/15

Meet Me Halfway

Being so spent
There is nothing more to give
Witnessing so much inwardly
Not able to live

Starting a movement
Without even a spark
Motivating the weary
Isn't a walk in the park

Having a vision
That's crystal, so clear
It's living in a world
Devoid of despair

Having a means
To achieve such a goal
Constantly refining my purpose
Redefining my role

Healing the multitudes
One at a time
Awakening humanity
Is surreal, sublime

The female embodiment
Gets in the way
Can't anyone recognize
Illusion at play

I have come here in prose
As best as I can
To ease the suffering of others
Uplift the consciousness of man

It can be done in an instant
An hour, or a day
If only each individual
Would meet me halfway.

You have a purpose
As sacred and true
To be the best possible
Version of you

10/2/16

Perceiving in Energy

You see an acorn
I see a tree
You make random statements
I hear a decree

You shed a tear
I see resolve
You feel the pain
I help it dissolve

You're counting down
To a final hour
I serve an infinite world
I strive to empower

You diminish the world
With your careless dismissal
Creating a world
That is fearful and abysmal

The God that you pray to
Is not up in the sky
It's in the face of your brethren
Toe to toe, eye to eye

When you're kind, thoughtful, caring
Your countenance is true
Goodness works through your intention
And all that you do

You're awakening to empowerment
Striving for peace for us all
Hear the music of Nature
Answer the call

Swim through the currents
That are graceful and kind
Speak well of all creatures
Unburden the mind

Give better than you get
Religiously too
This is the empowerment
Awakening in you

You are the seed
Of an amazing new realm
You navigate the ship
Your truth is the helm

Speak and be it now
In confidence and insight
You are the Love
You are the Light
4/10/16

Permission

There's nowhere to go
Nothing to do
No one to please
This day is for you

Nothing to conquer
Nothing to lose
This life is your oyster
It's yours to peruse

Freedom is yours
No need to ask why
Just put up your feet
And give it a try.
9/20/14

Sighting

The concave line on an inner circle
Parallel to the setting sun
Framed by the arch of myth or legend
An oblique sighting of "what could have been"

The brightest star in the farthest dimension
Waving whimsical and free
Was it in a dream or aspiration
I recognize that star as me.

The Expounded Moment

Whatever you are doing...
Savor it like that first bite after a long hunger
Be as transfixed by it as the final game of your team and its rival
Anticipate it like the first kiss of a love at first sight
Prolong it like a dreaded goodbye of a kindred spirit
Dote on it like your long anticipated first newborn
Get lost in it like the life's accomplishment of your favorite
author
Escape in it like an exotic second honeymoon
Stroke it like a purring long haired kitten

Be as enthralled in it as your favorite childhood hobby

Revere it as the snooze five on a Monday morning

Revel in it as your tired head would that soft pillow

Immerse yourself in it like your favorite new release

Taste it with your raw unguarded emotions

Touch it with the wisdom of your earnest heart

Scrutinize it with the clarity of your ever awakening spiritual eye

Hear it immersed with the inner strains of a celestial song

Echo it throughout your aligned incorporated being

Emanate it through the sacredness of everything you hold dear

Be it in every exaggerated engaged way

Expound upon it with the kindest intention

Awaken to the deliberate, conscious continuity of Celebrated Love

Make it your mainstay

Make it your "go to"

Immerse with it

Take it over

Make it you.

7/13/14

Thrill Ride

Come ride through the Universe with me
Upon a band of Light
Let go of all the burdens
That preclude you from this flight

Make a claim to your passage
Buy a ticket at the moment's gate
Where infinite love ebbs and flows
And perpetual miracles await

Come ride the wind and Light and Sound
Watch love flicker through the trees
Taste joy as dewdrops on your tongue
Feel your freedom in the breeze

Come scale the heights of eternity
Then drop through heaven's floor
All the wonders you wish to await you
Are within, as is so much more

Let's ride through eternity together
On the back of a midnight dream
Realizing every hurt, shame, or bruise
Is never what it may seem

Our pain is part of the adventure
That adds to the thrill of the ride
In the adventure of pure unadulterated love
Your true self has nothing to hide.
6/18/15

Between the Stillness and the Sky

I met myself one peaceful night
On glass ice dusted with snow
I awoke from a paralyzing stupor
To tell me what I needed to know

Others will find me inferior
This life will be my cruelest test
That I'll be admonished, humiliated and scorned
All while I am trying my best

It told me that life wasn't about being fair
That that was a quaint little notion
My ego will be literally pulverized
My spirit will nearly be broken
The pleasures that others live for
For me would be hard to attain

Every hope and desire will be stripped clear away
'Til my true self is all that remains

I told myself this to prepare me
As solace for the upcoming years
The real me knew what lay waiting ahead
The loneliness, anguish and tears

The real me gave me compassion
As I walked silently under the stars
It was the me that saw the whole picture
The journey, the struggle, the scars

I felt that kindness within me
A wisdom that dwelt deeper than pain
It gave me the love to endure knowing
Someday It'd be the only me to remain

Whenever I'm lost, alone or afraid
Or feel like I'm living a lie
I know I can always find my true self
Between the stillness and the sky

2/6/15

What Is a Poem?

What you call a poem, I think of as loving winged intention. Set to penetrate the defensiveness of the weary foot soldier. Piercing through to the deepest layer of apathy. Splitting open its dense hull and bursting the heart open. Just like a spontaneous bloom cracks open its pod and spills love everywhere in its wake.

A New Person

I am a new person each moment
The one I am at the core
I am more free, lighter and happier
Than I was just a moment before

I can sing my own praises
I can dance in the mist or the rain
I can embrace every tragedy
As it teaches me to let go of the pain

I can actually swim with the fishes
Even if it's in my own mind
I commune with the dolphins, whales and the seals
As I leave all illusion behind

I continuously consult with my mentors

The long-standing wisdom of trees

They tell me the truth that men no longer speak

They send it to me on the breeze

I can withstand almost anything

Loss, loneliness, the plight of our youth

But I can't wear the lies of this world

I no longer will bury my truth

Which is...

You are a mystery waiting to reveal

You are the answer you seek

Open yourself up and just look inside

Whatever you tell you, just speak

Sing it to all who will listen

Knowing much will fall on a deft ear

But it is so worth the performance

If even one note reaches someone to hear.

Love's Final Decree

Wait out the pain

It does have an end

Like looking up at the clouds for the rain to descend

Let it drip through your hair

And fall to the ground

As the force of the break

Reverberates and resounds

Crack open the nut

Where the anguish was held

Pull out the shriveled meat

That caused you such dread

Recover your composure

From that punch in the gut

No, you aren't shattered

You're still the whole nut

Recover your dignity

Walk away clean

You are guided in all endeavors

By forces unseen

Refute the notion

That you go it alone

You are honored as sacred

There's no sin to atone

Let the silence and loneliness

Cut through the facade

Rip through layers of bullshit

As the angels applaud

What you hold dear

As your own private hell

Drives you to hear truth

As clear as a bell

As Truth now personified

To this we agree

To hold space in this world

For Love's final decree.

11/9/15

Won't You Dance With Me?

I Am Soul

An unadulterated atom of breathtaking Love

Existing in a sea of pure bliss

Yet to become aware of myself in the higher worlds, I created movement

I acknowledged myself as a frequency of sound woven together with an emanation of light

I now knew how to maneuver the light by riding the sound

Joyful!

Yet I wanted to realize everything that I already knew

I decided to go into the most coarse vibrations

I delved down into the arenas of the mind

Everything was confusing

I got disoriented as thought matter collected upon me

I could not tell the difference between these thoughts and myself

They were now my identity

I kept going into denser existence

I saw experiences that were harsh and incredulous

But somehow thrilling

What was this thing collecting on me that made pain and trauma feel exhilarating

I wanted to see more and more of it

I kept going into darker regions

These things collected on me that made me react so inconsistently

Crying, Screaming, Anger, Pain, they seemed to bring anguish to me yet were fascinating

These capabilities became a part of me, I could control them or not

It was exciting at first to experience how such coarse matter expresses itself

I went to the most harsh vibration possible

It encased me in a tomb of flesh

There was little movement, no expansiveness

It was like being imprisoned in a sarcophagus

The only movement now came in the sporadic, inconsistent bursts of emotion

The woven tapestry of light and sound was encased in layers of dross matter

All seemed hopeless

The one saving grace was the heart

It seemed that the only way to forget how imprisoned I was, was to love

It wasn't easy because everything else was encased in course matter, too

But when I was able to show thoughtfulness to another, it allowed me access to more freedom

Love was so difficult

All those encased in their flesh tombs were in the same predicament

To get themselves free, two souls agreed to love the other person to create freedom for them

It worked

Loving another seemed to be the key

Wonderful!

This worked for eons

But souls got complacent

They flitted around making agreement with others to love them and leaving others behind

This created more great pain and more lessons

Sometimes two original souls kept their agreement

They are called soul mates

Sometimes they got separated and then life became about searching for them instead of realizing how to love

In a desperate attempt to get free, souls tried to love themselves to get themselves free

There was no loss or let down...only the programming of unworthiness to break through

I found that when I loved all others, I loved myself more

And when I loved myself I was able to love all others as well

I realized that when I loved, I was no longer lonely, I felt connected

Indeed, I was connected to all others!

All the thoughts and feelings and inertia fell away

I was liberated

Now I am still in the coarse matter but with a purpose

I have a sense of whom I am as an atom of love ensconced in light and sound

My purpose is to help everyone realize themselves as an atom of love as well

To love them beyond their own capacities to realize who they are as soul

To free them all by loving them all

And in turn helping them realize the freedom and liberation of loving other souls

This is who I am today

This is who you are

We are greater than our emotions and mightier than our thoughts

We are more expansive than any experience we use to define ourselves

We are woven tapestries of light and sound interweaving in a dance of blissful joy

As more and more awaken to love the dance becomes more exhilarating

With every post, every exchange and every outpouring of love comes the unspoken request...

Won't you dance with me?

Life's Equation

You are the sum of all your experiences
Heartache, desire and glory bracketed by lifetimes
Multiplied by resilience
Compiled in a form as limiting as a number

You are the ultimate resolve
Pooled and planted in the illusion of one form
The vastness and fortitude of God limited only by your ability
To realize your own depth

You fraction your own greatness in relation to your acceptance
level
Your greatness is the whole number
Acceptance is the common denominator
You are exponential Love.

The Awakened

Truth withdrew into the mist
As ignorance blew its one last kiss
Many receded with the tide
To wait for "power" to subside

A few stood strong in soul's dark night
To help the wounded retake flight
They stood with backs against the wind
Waiting for the darkness to rescind

Control is the boil on power's decree
Brokers and pawns vestige their one last plea
Fear, anger, jealousy is their stance
To manipulate who leads in the final dance

Many awaken in the final round
Many more warriors start to rebound
Those that were fractured beyond compare
Spontaneously heal and start to repair

The wind is mild, the current is right
For the multitudes to take flight
They pull away from power's last try
Join the legion of awakened into the sky.
4/25/14

You Exponentially

Energy doesn't flow
Up and down
It churns everywhere
All around

You don't need to get
From here to there
You exist
Everywhere

You don't need to juggle
Things to do
Just stand in your center
They will rotate to you

We don't march through life
Soldiers of time
We are Children of Universe
The new paradigm

We are expressive, creative
Dynamic and free
We are everything to everyone
We imagine ourselves to be

We live beyond the concepts
Of birth, pain or death
We are as free as a windfall
Expansive as breadth

Open your horizons
To all that you are
Not a pile of flesh
But a perpetual star

Blazing in glory
Beyond even the sky
Stop wondering WHO you are
And start asking why

Like why are you so determined
To play it so small
Why don't you dance in the heavens
Heed the ethereal call

Why not realize yourself
Exponential and free
This is the "You"
You came here to be.
10/14/16

Crossing

Shed one last tear
Watch it drop slowly
On the dross and pain you thought were you

Say a short prayer over the remains
The crumpled casing
That you unzipped and walked out of

Say goodbye to the embarrassment and defilement
Which were your lessons
Fling yourself into the realms beyond The Milky Way

Make haste...or not
Time is merely a hiccup of a memory
Of the limitation you once adopted as you

Feel free
If you still need to feel...
Or, just choose to Be.
11/1/13

For All

What are you manifesting for yourself this moment?

What are you manifesting for others by default?

Are you supporting their highest aspirations?

Or are you telling them to play it safe?

Are you telling them to have a plan B insinuating that plan A will fail?

Are you causing it to fail by dampening their enthusiasm?

Are you telling your children to play it safe?

Are you training them to conform to a life that is less fulfilling but has less risk?

How did that work out for you?

Is your every desire satisfied and are you blissfully happy?

If not, why not support something grander for those you love?

Do you talk to the trees?

Do you keep wise council with yourself?

Do you look at the stars and remember all the countless lifetimes you looked up at these same stars?

Do you remember lifetimes of other stars? Perhaps two suns and many moons?

Do you secretly wish to return to a world you fleetingly remember?

Do you dismiss the beauty of the earth because you lament the rugged treatment of being brought here many lifetimes ago?

Do you miss your native planet so much that you forget your own joy?

Nostalgia is sweet. But is it worth missing the present?

Do you cry inside for a pain that you don't remember?

Do you ache for a love you have never felt the touch of in this life?

Are you hell bent on making yourself miserable?

Do you allow your hopes and dreams to be dashed by a synthetic reality of earthly time and the illusion of age?

When is the last life you walked into the forest and felt yourself among kindred spirits?

When did you stop talking to nature and the trees?

When did it become okay to randomly kill life forms that were inconvenient?

When did man become so superior?

Did it coincide with the birth of ignorance?

You determine your own dynamo by the depth of your insights

It is a choice to swim shallow

Perhaps the pain has overtaken you and you are still cramped up from the blow

But you are still whole...you have all raw essence

Stake a claim in who you are...who you are meant to be

You are indeed entitled, but not in earthly trinkets

You are entitled in the depth and the wealth of the knowledge of the true self

You own a personal blueprint to your empowerment

Take as many with you along the way

Trudge out a cow path to a new adventure

Lead the way

Love the way

Beckon all to the way

Bless those on the wayside as well

Everyone is empowered, so leave a trail of bread crumbs

Trust others to forge a way through their own dreams and
insights

As you call along for them as you go

Calling in the joy and depth of abundance

For all...

For all.

Encouragement

Don't be afraid to dirty the knees

Or get gravel embedded in the palm of each hand

When scaling beyond the highest limitation

Leap into the greater you

Walk across the bridge between wonder and belief

Stand in absolute "knowing"

That the gnawing ache that churns the stomach with grout

Beats back the spewing lies of "fear"

That mocks

Of the danger of adopting a new found freedom

Each leap between "belief" and "realized"

Is jumping beyond the pay scale of convention

Your dreams are the expansion of the bigger stroke you use

When actualizing the brush of your own potential

Let the butterflies free

Give them girth

The bigger your attempts

The wider their wing span

The grandest intentions

Risk the greatest drop into the abyss

Yet the gap is necessary for your own awakening

Every "try" strengthens the muscles of conviction

Every fail is a success

The real danger is laying curled up in indifference

With the curtains closed to your own potential

7/25/14

Dreams

Dreams are us processing our lessons

As our soul body dances through air

If you notice me dancing along

It's only to show you I care

Sweet dreams everyone

See you on the other side of the veil

May you know how deeply you truly are loved

As you see Joy, Abundance and Freedom prevail.

Bonded in Purpose

I am the sinner

I am the saint

I am the canvas

I am the paint

I am a rocket

Also, its spire

I am the tinder

I am the fire

I am every experience

There possibly could be
I am the forest
I am each tree

I am all secrets
Carried upon the wind
I ride each new wave
As I watch them rescind

I am the echo
The tremble of each leaf
I exemplify each truth
Emotion, belief

I get inside you
You get inside me
We are together
Everything that can be

We are the whisper
The reckoning of each truth
The salty old wise one
The arrogance of youth

We crack our pods open
In this seedbed of life

We blurt out each wonder
We lament every strife

We are humanity
Coming to a head
The young virgin bride
Being led to her bed

We'll awaken disheveled
With new knowing eyes
Truth will be naked
To our glorious surprise

We'll know the id
Of our lonely desires
Was a prompting to greet
What now transpires

The introduction of love
In an expansive new way
We are now bonded in purpose
In the dawn of each day.

Any Day

Any new day is a sacred occasion
Any ole day is a benchmark to mark
Any new day is the first day of summer
Any day is a new dog's first day in the park

Any day is a day to give thanks and worship
A labyrinth, adventure, new season or birth
Any day is a great one to behold and to treasure
Any day is the best one to be here on earth

Any day is the dawn of a clear new perspective
Glorious, exhilarating, reverent and new
Any day is how I want to spend my forever
Any day is every day when I spend it with you.
- Jen Ward and Tree 10/25/14

A Series of Blessings

The deep dark abyss
Between reality and truth
The lack of awareness
In the decrepit or youth

The mucus thin sheath
Between real and illusion
An amniotic connection between
Pain, joy, and their fusion

An ill equipped fledgling
An adept old sage
Both play their parts handsomely
On life's Shakespearean stage

Wisdom accumulates through lifetimes
Never as a flash in the pan
Lightning doesn't strike more than just once
But experience can

Again and again
We meet death as our fate
Carry over our lessons
To the next embryonic state

Ignorance or bliss
Can repeat verse for verse
Life can be a series of blessings
Or a perpetual curse

One key factor
That rings as clear as a bell
We make our own heaven
Or live our own hell

It all depends
On what we see or deny
Will we ground ourselves in concepts
Or let ourselves fly

The choice is the "you"
You are willing to be
Grounded in fear
Or loving and free.

Loneliness

Embrace loneliness for what it is
Love calling from afar
Depression, angst and disappointment
False emanations from a star

For how can light be anything
But beautiful and serene
Believing you're anything but vibrant and love
Leaves depths of you unseen

You are amazing as you always will be
There's no point in arguing this truth
You are always as free and expansive
As light, beauty, abundance and youth

Step away from the discouragement...
The clouds that hide your light
They muddled your mind unintentionally
Hindering the consciousness of your flight

See truth for what it really is...
You stepping into yourself
Open the door to your own inner worlds
That fear and indifference put on a shelf

You are wonder fully awakening
A blossom ready to perch into song
This transient world is not your true home
The heart of love is where you truly belong.
4/26/15

The Rainbow's Muse

If someone tells you a lie
Use it to discern your truth

If someone tells you that you're ugly
Show the world how beautiful you really are

If someone tells you that you're wrong
Prove to yourself that you are right

If someone stomps on your dreams
Breathe life into them with your wonder

If someone tries to discredit you
Let your integrity and grace discredit their claim

If someone tries to pull you into their quicksand

Hunker into your stance and reclaim your empowerment

If someone asks something of you in sincerity
Introduce them to the depth of their own capabilities

If someone tries to stroke your ego
Brush off their gross offense

Show them how to greet you
In the neutrality of Love's breathe
Emanate from within and reflect their light back to them
Whisper their greatness in the resonance of pure song
Lead them into the forever of a moment
As their own single strain of an ancient celestial song

This is why you have landed here
Not to be defeated in the illusion of pain
But to instill your loving essence on the "All of Life"
You are the wonder
You are the moonbeam's inspiration
You are the rainbow's muse

Don't you dare be defeated by the ignorance of a lie
Don't you crumble to a crumb of arrogance
Don't you dare desecrate such marvel with self-indulgence
You are part of a greater vision

Accept your status in the eternal state of wonder
With the maturity of an aware lens
Align yourself perfectly with the dance of each atom and planet

And find your own rhythm and pace with love...
In all that you do.

Encouragement of a Full Moon

Stand between the sun and moon
Let the love and light pass through
Illuminate your bountiful heart
Drop the extraneous part called you

Magnify your bountiful heart
To the size and width of earth
Treat it as a looking glass
To show others their ultimate worth

Hold up the mirror to their giant group heart
Brace as they cringe and recoil
Pour love into the very essence of all
Drain all the dross out into the soil

Hold the reflection steadily
Ignore the negative onslaught
Love breezes clean every last atom
Before its true essence is caught

Be unwavering as the moon and the sun
Match their luminescent light
Allow others to realize the brilliancy of truth
By accessing their own second sight

Span across the globe of man
Rise above the stagnant air
Pierce the earth with your magnified love
Let it feel the extent of your care.

Become one with the body of earth
Let the sun and moon's light pass straight through
Expand the atoms to an omniscient state
Allow truth to align in you

Be the surrogate of the highest purpose
In the humanity of man
Yes it's possible to help the world transcend
Just by believing you can.

Soul Trail Blazer

Cast a net upon the shore
Let it rest upon the surface
Draw it back with mindful regard
Of its duality of purpose

Draw abundance to yourself
Let gratitude be its drag
Others churn in overt waters
Their curses are their plague

Leave behind the gritty bitters
The natural backwash of the brew
Say grace over the elixir
Something others fail to do

Etch your name upon the table
Soft wood kept under glass
Leave a note for the next soul traveler
In a weatherworn sealed flask.

Homage to the Foliage

Hear the tiny million voices
From all the world around
Feel the little advocates
And the blessings that abound

Perceive their angst
And plight to thrive
Know their calling
"I Am Alive"

Perceive them crying
To be seen...
"I am not human...
But I am green"

Sense them linger
In your heart
"We are not separate

We do our part"

Acknowledge their gift
Show you care
"We are your breath

We make your air

"We make life pretty

We heal your stress

When you're with us

You worry less

"We buffer sounds
That are too harsh
We bring the stillness
Of the marsh

"We help all people
Quietly refrain...
From collectively
Going insane"

So thank your flowers,
Your grass, a tree
They make us all
A better "me."

Abundance

Pierce the pale sheath of laden indifference
Examine its contents with the scrutiny of an expectant heart
Live way beyond the meagerness of your perceived means
Dive head first into the ample bosom of your true wealth

Brush the stray strands from your limited view
Wipe away sweat and unfurrow the brow
Tilt your visor to support the view
See your abundance dancing off the horizon...

Will her closer
And at all costs...
Take her in.

Falling to Sleep

Within walls of solitude
Subtle imagery comes to me true
Hallucinations? Thoughts? Feelings of God?
Questioning everything of what I once knew

I leave the body
I AM unbound
Silence echoes
Saturated sound

An unhindered spirit
A vessel of light
I explore the universe
All through the night.

Contemplation

Within walls of solitude
Subtle realities come to be true
Imagery, thoughts, feelings of God
Whispering Its name, the sacred Hu

I leave the body, I AM unbound
Silence saturated, echoes sound
Love that's incredible, it's all around
Motionless expulsion as soul journeys home.

Sighting

The concave line on an inner circle
Parallel to the setting sun
Framed by the arch of myth or legend
An oblique sighting of "what could have been"

The brightest star in the farthest dimension
Waving whimsical and free
Was it in a dream or aspiration?
I recognize that star as me.

Butterfly

Reclaim the succor of abandonment

A wild child foraging on expectation

The eagerness of a bloated salesman perched to close the next deal of a lifetime

The "girl next store" just discovering the power of her womanhood

A shy man's baritone musings at the memory of the first crack of his new voice

Expect every door to open to miracles

Unzip that last tooth of an outdated purpose

Shred that last fiber of the last thread of an outdated cocoon

Unfurl the new you unhindered by expectations

Dangle your feet high above the heads of judgment

Fly away!

Motives

Motives are transparent
Like concentric rings on a still pond
With one emanating intention
To the naked eye seems selfish
Notice me
Give to me
See my importance
But the compassionate looks deeper
See me
I have been ignored, abandoned, rejected, defiled
Notice me
So I no longer wander alone as an apparition
Recognize me
So that I know that I exist
Give to me
I have been starved to emaciation
Robbed of all I hold dear
Stripped to the bone
Raped and left crumpled in the dirt
Give to me so I can clothe my shame
Give to me to so I can bind and balm my wounds
Give to me so I can rest on a pile of false pride
Until I can endure more of the journey to my true self
See me
See me so I can feign strength
See me so I can shake off the haughty mocking from within
See me so I can anchor myself in relationship to you

See me so I can wade through the myriad of shame that
accompanies me

Yes, the compassionate eye looks past the ripples

Into the depth of the stillness of the pond

It sees pure intention that is too shy to try

Innocence that has lost its way

Truth that has gone mute

Compassion acknowledges these

Encourages pure intention

Empowers innocence

Speaks with truth in the ancient tongue of stillness

Heals a heart

Heals a land

Heals their own self-inflicted wounds, heals all.

We

We are not our physical form

A mere structure made out of mortar and bricks

A building doesn't laugh or bleed or dream

Emotions are not extreme weather to a fragile house

There's no need to batten down the hatches

In fear of being destroyed by a good cry

Our thoughts are not meant to govern us

They are not taxes or a speed trap

We are not on perpetual parole

We are fluid and free, spontaneous and light
A fickle butterfly resting lightly in our physical form
And flitting away on our laughter and our whims...

Into a perpetual dream.

Meditation

Intake a legion of stillness
Bow to each atom as it enters the gateway of your beingness
Accept each offering of bliss
Carry the love through your inner transport
Breathe bounty into the weary trenches
Receive the message from your true essence
Beyond the confines of your physical form
Embrace the awakening of inner dialogue
With which thoughts cannot betray
Accept the love beyond all reason
See waves of light emanate from your orb
Feel with your true heart
Know beyond the mind
Replenish the resolve to love beyond all measure
Awaken in your true form...the formless.

Nameless One

What do I call you?

Not a word that the multitudes use to curse others
Father?
My father disappointed and abandoned me
Lord?
Kings have been using that word for eons to wield power
That is not you
Holy Ghost?
This conjures up the image of lost souls...
Trinity?
A trendy girl's name
All words diminish the depth of your being
So how do I define you?
With a simple spontaneous smile given and received a thousand times a day
How do I revere you?
By disturbing the tranquility of your stillness as little as possible
And sharing the gifts that you have allotted me...
With gratitude
May every moment be an homage to you.

Outwitting Pain

Be the sore thumb of humanity
Be Waldo and find yourself
Stab conformity in the throat and render it speechless
Blur the lines between the self and genius

Namaste the genius in all

Pain—the unfulfilled efforts
To subjugate truth
Aligning strands of misnomers
Into a faux-fibered synthetic reality

Based on fears and betrayal
Of the ultimate power
Of innocence
Over the dross

Remnants of the dark ages
Re-gathered into piles of moss
To fertilize the organic law
So as to taint truth

Pain is the schism
Created between
The ultimate self
And a pseudo reality

Throbbing is the echo
Into the cavern between them
Loneliness is dropping a pebble into the depths
Yet not hearing the completion of its fall

Only unadulterated love
The fluid of the angels
Can suture where the bridge is
To heal the self from within.

When

If not peace......What?
If not now......When?
If not to uplift......Why?
If not with love......How?
If not here......Where?
If not you......Who?

Want

Want is throwing your line to the farthest reaches of the galaxy and expecting it to land a prize--while all along you are standing on the X where the treasure is buried.

Hope

"Faith" and "Hope" are the twin sisters
Waiting to meet their charming prince
"Knowing" is the true bride
Who adorns the moment with her splendor
—Accepting her intended at her feet
Where the sacred altar of love resides.

Break Out

Bust the clay pot you've been planted in
Finger-walk your roots deep into the ground
Unfurl your layers under the North Star
Reach between the east and west winds
Awaken your primal purpose.

A Portal of God

To dance upon the horizon all through the night
To live in the exhilaration of an eagle's first flight

To pursue a purity all others abscond
To breathe in each moment forever and beyond

To dive into the heavens as your own private pool
To see life from the vantage point of a perpetual school

To be the Lover, the Teacher, the Healer of man
Living in the moment where all ends and began

To rise to the surface of humanity's cream
To support each being's purpose—their intimate dream

To cheerlead all others and actually applaud
Is the moment you become a portal of God.

Flashpoint

How do you know that:
The next altruistic act
Serendipitous encounter
Grandiose epiphany
Rant
Cry
Struggle
Simple act of kindness
Quiet resolve
Sincere smile
Honest self-reflection
Is not the flash point
That uplifts all of humanity
With its purity of intent
And alignment to the moment?

Self-Realization

Readjust your magnetic north
Circumnavigate your inner potential
Wax and wane without thought of
Loss or gain

Regroup from the ebb
Throw yourself back into the flow
Decompose all conception of loss

Re-fertilize your field of insight and acceptance

Transcend the concepts of fear, pain, limitation
Gather all possibilities into the moment of now
Beyond the inhale and exhale of hope's expectation
Ease gracefully into your own omnipotence.

True Journey

When life brings problems...it teaches resilience

When everything is taken away...it shows how little is truly needed

When everyone walks away...one becomes self-reliant

When no one is around to love...love reveals itself in every crevice

When thoughts are stifling...one finally learns to disengage from them

When the whole world seems insane...it reveals the simplicity of truth

When the heart feels broken...it is ego that takes the blow

When there is loss through death...the illusion of separation is revealed

When one cries out in anguish...the soul celebrates the freedom

When one gives up...the true journey begins.

Healers Reunite

An echo fills the ancient sky, there's heard one universal cry

Percussions, movement, a rhythmic blend, hands that heal, bodies mend

The dance to capture visions lost, regain freedom at all cost

Broken lives we all endure, remembering wholeness is the cure

To wash away the ills of man, unite us with our tribe again

In this life few understand what the Shaman can withstand

To ease the suffering of those she can, heart to heart and hand to hand

Eons later old friends dispersed to meet as strangers is the curse

Ways of remembering now dull and gray, all searching for the easy way

The healer steps forward in the artificial light to show the brilliance of true sight

Ancestors dance with spirits of earth and wind

Enhance the process of remembering

All seekers of truth squint to see, the humble stance of the Shaman's decree

As she summons the spirits, blows away the pain

Calls love back to the earth again

With the bending of the light, others break through to night

Remembering their vows to reunite

As coaches and healers they re-gather their clan

Inspired to mend the broken land

We meet again across time and space, see recognition in a weary face

A fellow healer who endured at all cost

And many times thought that all was lost

Feel the blessings that do ensue when one lost crusader learns there's two

Exponential healing has begun

Spiritual freedom is now re-won!

Family

Sometimes I feel alone but I'm not
For look at the wonderful family I've got
Do I need them?
Well, yes quite a lot
For without them where would I be?

I'd be in the middle of a motionless sea
Or in a dark dungeon which long lost its key
Life would be meaningless
Don't you agree?
For who can survive all alone?

A hermit dies with an embittered tone
Did he really choose to live life alone?
Will anyone visit when he's laid with the stone?
I don't think so
And neither does he.

So count your blessings one by one
From mother to sister to father to son
When you've finished and the counting is done
Start over...
And count them again.

- Jen Ward at age 9, her first poem.

The Cycle of You

A manifestation of a pure expression
Emanating from a blend of light and sound
A breath from an ancient source
Forming a parabola from an ethereal wand
That bubbles to form
A pure loving intention
A compilation of experiences and memories
A vibrant ball of emotional energy
Rolling upon itself
Building in intensity...
Until it bursts forth
To be encapsulated in a casing of flesh
You are a dream manifested
Once you were subjective
Until you, enmeshed in the tangible worlds of matter, energy,
space, And time
Weighted down by their illusions
Wistful of the winged expression of "You" before form
The embedded purity of divine love
Always speaking in your ear
With ultimate truth tugging at your heart chords
Biding time, building stamina
Consciously lightening your repertoire
Heaving away chunks of illusion
Until the "You" transcends the mundane indifference
Make light of your presence
Song of your essence

—

Emanate from within
Carry yourself away on one simple strain of melodious love
Into the higher realms
As a Conscious Soul.

Conviction

Eyes sometimes blur
But still can see
Minds can be imprisoned
But remain totally free
Bones that are broken quickly mend
A will with conviction will never bend
Hearts can love stronger after they break
Dreams are remembered right before wake
Whispers are heard by leaning in
God is discovered by tuning within.

What Would Dr. Seuss Say?

You think I am there
And you are here
But you are there
There is here
We are here
Here is now
We are in
The Here and Now

You think I'm great
And you are small
That makes no sense
No sense at all
How can it be when I am you
We are the same
Just one
Not two

As a fact, we are all one
It's always been
Since life's begun
We are not separate
You and me
We are the same
We are the we

The world is made of

One big we
We span the globe
This we that's me
When you are hurt
We feel the same
We cry and stomp
And give out blame

We defend ourselves
Exhaust our wits
Stomp about
In angry fits
But when we perch
To strike a blow
Then's the time
We need to know

When we hurt them
We hurt the we
I hurt you
You hurt me
Let's turn the tables
On this game
Disarm the drones
And refrain

When you want
To hate yourself
See me crying

On a shelf
When you want
To say you're bad
Realize
You've just been had
The hate you give...
To your me
Is the plight
Of the universal we

If you want to
Heal the all
Crumble that
Inner wall
The wall that says
You can not be
Wonderfully abundant, happy, free.

I Wish...

I wish you could see you through my eyes

To acknowledge the incredible beauty that you truly are

I wish you could drop the ugly layers of defenses

Or the habit to run away

I wish you would let go of all pretenses that kept you safe so many lifetimes

Know all enemies as merely friends with their own set of defenses

I wish you would stop clinging to problems and pain

Hooking them to yourself with the possessive word "my"

I wish you could let go of the fear that is obliquely fed to you by others

And habitually tapped into your veins

Wean yourself off it

Forgo the drama of elusive illusion blowing around in the mind and settling in the heart

Break through the sac of false pride

Bash through to the love and allow it to gush free

Searing through the shackles that have stained your grace

Relax in being un-shelled

Accept the raw skin feeling of the unencumbered you

Gather up the love from within and wrap yourself in its depth

Throw it over your head so that you can see yourself with Love's eyes

Feel the love with Love's heart

Know yourself with Love's mind

And dissolve all dregs of separation.

Awakening

Break through that glazed facade
Penetrate the thick layers of hardened mucus
That eras of devastation forged into deadbolts
More tended than the encasing on a grain of sand
That disturbs the haven of a mollusk's inner sanctum
Dip that ladle in the sanctity of the infinite well
Exposed memories now sting to the core like a foreboding song
Allow them to bleed out
They shock the numb casing to relinquish its glory
Acerbating the isolation with a haunting strain
Craving a love that is a sunset away...or worse
A mistaken glimpse of what could have been
The memory of which hits the nerve circuit like a splinter
wedged under a nail
Every shell must be broken, each gosling must cut free
Every loss and devastation is a hammer to the shell they
themselves built
Eventually spilling out the love
A beautiful and messy birth of the awaited arrival
Awakening takes its first breath
A new heart beats against the backdrop of the absolute
Love unfurls its sapling wings
Catching a hint of a breeze of an absolute truth
Migrates into the dawn of new era.

Your Joy

Toss your atoms into the ethers
Catch them on the wind
Scatter them beyond all reason
Where time and space begin

Throw your voice into the sky
To worlds beyond the night
Follow it to that ageless place
Where your true self first took flight

Twirl and revel in your joy
Dance partner with a star
Realize the personified love
That you really are.

Love's Best Lesson

I gave away my power
It was easy, I confess
Someone smiled sweetly
Then I was possessed

I have been stripped bare to the bones
And know there are many more
That in their desperate need to love
Became an open door

Were plundered, raped, soiled, and spurned
Mangled, broken, and deprived
But 'cause of their ability to love
Managed to survive

Now's the time to make things whole
By pulling back all our parts
With dignity and grace intact
We repair all broken hearts

By teaching when we take from others
We are stealing our own grace
Everyone else is merely the self
Reflected in another face

And when we give too easily
We weaken the whole in all
Yet when we help another
We are answering our own call

We have learned love's best lesson
When we finally believe
We give the most to the all
When we confidently receive.

How?

How could someone so beautiful
Be so unaware
To see the worthiness in everyone else
But with themselves pretend not to care?

How could someone shine with such love
Be blinded to such a degree
That they see what they see bursting in others
Yet in themselves they refuse to see?

How can someone share such incredible gifts
Encouraging all others in receiving
But when it comes to their dynamic self
Have trouble even believing?

How do you encourage someone
Who's hell-bent on besmirching
The magnificent fountain of love they are
And that they are the source they're searching?

How do you make someone realize
To clearly understand
That while they are being loving to all
They are holding themselves in remand?

How can you pin them up against truth
That they are reflecting so clear

To make them know the incredible beauty
They are reflecting themselves in the mirror?

How about writing a long winded poem
That resonates responsibly true
That the person this poem is definitely about
Is the one reading it now. It is you!

Acknowledging the Journey

We have all been beaten down
Tortured for speaking up
Killed for standing out
Sacrificed for being beautiful
Challenged for being strong
Humiliated for being different
Starved, hanged, drowned,
Murdered, abandoned, and rejected.

It is amazing that we have anything left in us
But we do
It may be a matter of just tapping into that place
That has not been manipulated
Deceived
Used up
We may have to crawl into that pure pooled place within
ourselves
Splash it on our face.

Revive ourselves enough...
To drink from the infinite well
If we can't do it for ourselves
We can do it for each other
Until we are all standing in our empowerment
We are all whole,
Abundant,
Loving and free.

Section II: Life

Love's Own Decree

I don't fall on my knees
Pray up to the sky
Condemn others as sinners
With a self-righteous sigh

I don't follow man's rules
As if all are golden
I don't covet a church
To which I'm beholden

I don't sing the praises
Of an old man in a robe
There are too many discrepancies
When I start to probe

I'm not a dutiful soldier
Doing what I'm told
I hold myself accountable
When I am worn out and old

I don't sit on the sidelines
Terrified to sin
I participate in life

Whether I lose, draw or win

I'd rather be wrong
And live life so bold
Than be the hero in a story
That's never been told

I'd rather see God smiling in the eyes
Of a man, dog or tree
Then condemned to a heaven
That no one wants to be

It'd be a gilded cage
With no compassion or gain
This is not me
It's a fate I'd disdain

Let me get my hands dirty
Loving all in the now
It's no stranger than having 72 virgins
Or worshiping a cow

Instead of seeing God
In a void, out in space
I'd rather know God now
In every beautiful face

Look God in the eyes
In the needy and old
To see God in everyone
Seems idealistic and bold

There's no stringent white heaven
For which I give a damn
I'm lost in a sea of imperfection
Merely claiming "I AM"

I am the lonely
I am the poor
I am the Jehovah's Witnesses
Who knock at my door

I relish the pain
I laugh at the wind
As I see God in everyone
I watch evil rescind

Self-righteous pride
Is the work of the Devil
It's better to be empowered
And see all at this level
The moral outcries

The war and the crime

They must all end now

They must stop on a dime

We all are empowered

Everyone must agree

When we see God in everyone

In the collective of we

I am your savior

You are my grace

We share the continuity of God

In the homeliest face

When we condemn or judge anyone

We are diminishing God

We must take the wrappings of religion

See through the facade

I don't judge you

Please don't condemn me

Superimpose benevolence upon me

Then just let me be

In the name of the Father

Son, Holy Ghost

God resides in all others

So love others the most

The Nirvana that you strive for

By doing your part

Is accessed by a gateway

From everyone's heart

We usher each other into heaven

By Love's own decree

Of me honoring you

As you respect me.

5/26/16

Love's Trail

We are not separate

Your fortitude runs through my body as the veins of my soul

Your heart beats in synchronicity with mine

When you ache, I feel your angst and cry your tears

I know your fears like a memory of sitting in sullied clothes

Until love washes it away with bleached white tears

I feel that place where you hold the welling of your hopes

I know the hesitancy to share

I see you playing it cool so no one will pop your bubble

Not realizing that the bubble is a false self

It needs to be bashed against life

So that the love can burst through the stark reality of your greatness

Splashing it back into your face

Waking you to know you are not great because of what you do

You are great because you try, strive, continue to be and thrive

Never ceasing to exist

Contemplate the miracle of your existence

Trace yourself back to beyond the invention of time and space

Dangle your feet on the edge of the Universe with me

Feel the freedom in resting beyond action

There is no need to validate your worth

Untie those edges that bind you to a life that does not reflect your wonder

Unshackle yourself from the need to earn...a wage, love, happiness, sense of belonging

Grasp the simple nature of love, your true self, your essence

Practice the ancient art of hand crafted kindness

Throw pots of joy off the wheel of life

Glaze them in your sincerity of intention

Know your true purpose no matter what illusion conditions you to believe

I see your dance, I see you stub your toe as easily as I feel my own limitation

Let's dance together with no one needing to lead

—

Let's whirl around in the exuberance of unabashed joy

Let's fall down laughing and help each other up

May we encourage all to curtsy and bow to a whimsical nature

Catch the breeze in their face as you blow kisses to the ether and feel them return in a gush of acceptance

You are the loving intention you put out in the world

You are not the lump of coal that watches it go

You follow it along love's trail

Until you realize that we are the path for each other

We are the blessed, the blessing and wherever it is bestowed

All this is within and without, in you and in me

In all we see and don't see

It is what is entailed in perpetually being

It is ours when we realize ourselves to be...

Unhindered, untethered, unencumbered and free.

6/7/15

Perspective from Intuitive Healer Jen Ward

Your worst...day may be...a day in the park to someone else

Your worst...meal may be...a banquet to someone else

Your worst...living conditions may be...a palace to someone else

Your...deepest disappointment may be...a dream come true to someone else

Your worst...date may be...a love of their life to someone else

Your...haziest stupor may be...a moment of clarity to someone else

Your...throw away attempt may be the...highest accomplishment to someone else

Your...failing body may be...renewed health to someone else

Your...fat pants may be...skinny pants to someone else

Your...bad luck could be...catching a break to someone else

Your...lack of gratitude...may be an insult to 90% of the planet.

Real Beauty

Stop using stilettos as a stepladder to be seen above the crowd
Wipe off the colored chemicals that mute your inner hue
Quit gluing fringe on the windows to the soul
Unzip the mask of denial that hides the real you

Lines are the road map to your wisdom and your mirth
How will one find you if you pull them tight
They are the crinkles and etchings of your charm
They are where your essence glows

They are your real beauty.

Silent Majority

I hate in any way, shape or form
Someone tells me what to be
It even makes me angry
To think that I'm not free

There are many different people
Who like to tell me I am wrong
But others who appreciate truth
Remark that I am strong

It feels like there are still some groups
That care what I believe
It's like they try to micromanage God
And how love is received

There are seven billion ways on earth
To worship and to pray
As many as that even seems
That number's growing every day

It doesn't really matter
What others tell you to do
After all is said and done
You'll still in fact be you

So mute the judgment in your mind

Of what you say, think, be, or feel

It's your own truth that needs listening to

It's the only one that's real

Take a leap towards freedom

For yourself and all the world

Step outside your comfort zone

Let your own voice now be heard

Advocate for animals

Speak openly to trees

Put your reputation out there

For whales, the impoverished and bees

There is a silent majority

That's gone deaf, dumb and mute

They cringe and they recoil

At the thought of any dispute

But the world has been uplifted

Seeds of war must quickly die

Every soul must now reclaim its wings

And remember how to fly.

The Example

The child who is given such little regard
That keeps to itself
Tries real hard

That researches life through every exchange
Cries to itself
Loves through disdain

The child who is taken less seriously
Gives of itself
So creatively

The child who is never given a second glance
Second helping
Or even a chance

The child who survives by flying under everyone's sight
Who has make-believe friends
Cries through the night

A child who grows weary of feeling the pain
Loves any little creature
To keep from going inside

This child should grow into a crotchety old coot

It's not that far-fetched

The point isn't moot

But somewhere, somehow love intervened

Kept this child safe

From a negative refrain

This child is adopted by nothing but grace

Though pain and its cousins

Show on its weary face

This child grows to adulthood

Ahead of the curve

To the chagrin of the haters who think they have nerve

Who does this child think that they are

To remain so intact

Smiling through every scar

This child knew that the suffering that their small body could take

Was best felt in them

Than to watch someone else ache

The child took the suffering and passed it right through

It was as if it was a mission
That they needed to do

This child is a survivor and so is anyone that can see
That the plight of all others lives in you
And in me

So take this child's example to pass through the pain
See it as a wisp of smoke leaving
And never a stain

It doesn't matter if your life looks like a success
Just continue to continue
And know you are blessed

For every challenge that you meet that doesn't sweep you away
Just take a deep breath
And call it a good day.
6/18/16

Jen Ward, RM, LMT

The Sisterhood of My Brethren

Be who you are at your center
The love, the light and the joy
Forgo the peripheral drama
That pretends to be you

Scrape off the carbuncles
Of want, need and desire
Pain is the twisted sinew
That wraps around your bones

Untether the twisted expectations
That cause you to hunch and recoil
Unfurl from the branded complacency
That aligns you to the limitations of flesh and time

You are the dreamer by choice
Fantasy is your launching pad
Each hopeful intention lobs you
Closer to the pinpoint of your potential

You are transformed beyond
The fathom of all naysayers
The sinister, the unforgiving
You arise to the surface of awakening

Let go of the struggle between your slumber
And the reality of your dreams
Forgo the need to struggle with those still asleep
Or have their permission for you to awaken

The Universe is spitting you out
Into the reality of your awakened self
Do not expect the placenta of the false world
To grow with you into your spiritual skin

You do it alone for a reason
You who are too giving will give credit to a false God
This is your journey...your celebration
There is no victory in giving over your power once again

All habits must die, all limitations ripped through
Like dry brittle husks waiting to blow away in the wind
Pay attention to your own arrival
As you marvel at the husk filled whirlwind about you

To arrive is your virtue and your honor
To be empowered is your new sheen
We have been waiting lifetimes to celebrate
Beyond the threshold of the limitations of duality

Dance your primal song as you watch

The vestige of the false self leave

You are your own savior

Humanity's golden child of a saving grace

A victor through the raging war of indifference

Ignorance, manipulations and lies

You are now truth personified

As love, kindness and virtue bleed beauty through your skin

And captures the altruistic unabashed self

Gleaning with empowerment

In a world we all prayed was a reality

When we were still conditioned in our primal ways

Thank you for enduring

And holding a place for love

Thank you for the ember of innocence

You held to your tiny protected breast

All those who embrace their empowerment

Ride now on the back of your victory

You are the Phoenix of yore

You are realizing this beyond the settling of the dust

Behold all the others making their way to love's sea

Like a billion tiny turtles sans the shell and the enemies

We all make this journey now

Conscious of the new awareness we all embody

You are my kindred Phoenix turtle friend

As we make this journey exponentially together

Love and truth are our kinsfolk now

And you...are the sisterhood of my brethren.

5/30/16

The Unpaid Greens

The soil is depleted my friends
We sent too many prayers up to the sky
And left nothing to honor the earth
To feed into the sprigs of our foliage

Our greens go through the motion
Growing unfulfilled, unappreciated
Their life force waning from indifference
Over-taxed by expectations

No one can give in the richness of their fullness
Without being replenished a bit for their sacrifice
Recycled and composted indifference
Is still indifference

The greens are so weary of the ego cries
"Grow for my pleasure, feed me, be beautiful for me"
"Sacrifice yourself to my service"
With no thought of gratitude in return

The greens are so weary of being slaves to our indifference
The world where the selfish believe they alone are king
Apathy tries to taint their sweet stems
As we burn, poison and rape the sacred soil around them

—

Thank goodness for the resiliency of the greens

As the man made God hogs all the prayers for himself

Those who have fed, warmed and enriched us

Go unpaid for their sacred service.

5/30/16

Transcendence

Beyond Godly borders on which nationality depends
Is the universal war cry for Humanity to transcend

All the etchings in marble, the writings in stone
Are left to remind us...we don't do it alone

Walls are not made to keep us living in fear
Instead, we uphold a vision for all to hold dear

Beyond the facade of what we all know
Is good versus evil going toe to toe

The same struggle that takes place between us and our brethren
Is reflective of what's fought between our hell and our heaven

The same battle that's fought in our family and home
Is the same that played out in Ancient Athens and Rome

The same selfish desires and pettiness of plans
Is seen a billion times over in the struggle of man

When we conquer our dreams, put the ego in check
Take a moment from the drama...take time to reflect

It is clearly visible that on which we depend

Is an illusion that evaporates once we transcend

Gravity

We all start our first incarnations as pure Love

But then things happened...

We got ignored

We lost our way

We felt abandoned

Gravity happened and we fell down

Then we started to trust the gravity more than the love

We focused on appeasing the gravity...

Rather than enjoying the freedom

We started to look down so as not to fall

Everyone started to look down

Everyone agreed that gravity was the highest power. We forgot the Love

It is programming and conditioning

It is time to release all the pain and scars from past lives

And just embrace the loving core we started out with

Look up

Look around

See each other

See the love in each other

Validate the love in each other

Release the pain in each other

Remember the Love

Remember who we are

Remember our natural state

Remember our home. Be the Love

Be home to others' unrest

Welcome them in

Melt the fear

Embrace yourself in them

See the Love in their eyes

See yourself

Recognize yourself

Rejoice.

"We Can"

My job as a human is simply to "Be"

Convert every experience in relationship to me

I'm every windfall, I'm every dream

I'm every ocean, I'm every stream

I'm every adventure that could possibly happen to "man"

I live with intention, I do what I can

I know that this potential shrinks when I "fear"

It goes totally dormant when I show I don't care

Indifference allows others who show a spark of appeal

To take potential from all, they cheat, lie and steal

So instead of being everything that floats on the breeze

They become the apocalypse, they become the disease

They stand on the sidelines, roped in by the fear

Too proud to speak or show that they care

They give away their power to all who walk by

The dictates of society sanction suffering inside

War, depression, and disease have become the norm

Cannabis and Xanax...the only port in the storm

People are tired, and broken, and worn down to the soul

Merely to be loved, happy and free is their most humble goal

It can happen if every embodiment of man

Steps up to the plate and says that, "I Can"

"I can" imagine my potential, I'll give it a try
I will show kindness to all without questioning why
"I can" express wonderment and speak it out loud
Declare my intention, send it off in the cloud

"I can" withdraw my involvement in the destruction of man
I am doing it now by saying "I can"
"I can return to my original heartfelt desire"
To live with integrity, contribute and inspire

"I can return to the wonderment happening within me"
I am every potential, I'm every tree
Also, being inspiring seems valid to do
I encourage YOUR greatness. You are everything, too

Empower yourself! Give "you" a hand
Bestow every kindness on "you" that you possibly can
When you give love to you, it's bestowed upon me
We are all in it together, Joyful, Loving and Free

We are the windfall happening to man
In this very moment by embracing, "We can."

10/2/14

Where Truth and Love Began

Speak in the language of the Gods
Unencumbered by the tongue
Dance your virile empowerment
A bastion of the young

Detach the talons of time and space
From the countenance of you
Shatter all disfiguring misnomers
From all you think, say, feel or do

Streamline your outer vision
All but kindness disallow
There's no need to ask questions
Your true self knows the "how"

Debunk all the illusion
Of the pettiness of life
Divorce the "want", "need", "greed" and "power"
Take contentment as your wife

Do these things to heal the wounds
Inflicted by the pettiness of man
Your journey is always in the moment
Where truth and love began.

That's What You Do

No one can touch your head
To make you feel sane
No one can talk you through
A whole life of disdain
No one can see your whole forest
They'll fixate on one tree
Or live your life for you
'Tell you just how to be
No one can pressure you
To be an agreeable peer
Not by stroking the ego
Or saying they care
No one can know
What it is like to be you
They can try to fathom
But they'll just misconstrue
No one can broach
The depths that you reach
Not by virtue, devotion
Or flowery speech
The path that you're on
You venture alone
So make it count for something
Make it your own

Take back all the power

You've strewn along the way

Collect it back up

You'll need it some day

You are the only expert

On what it's like to be you

Has anyone ever tried

To try on one shoe

Save your energy

For what lies ahead

As you forge your own way

Make your own bed

The love that propels you

Comes from only one source

The Universe itself

Has sanctioned your course

So don't play it small

Or cower to the masses

They can't see your greatness

Not even with glasses

You will fall through the cracks

Your sense of pain will be heightened

You'll feel like a failure

Until you're enlightened

The path then won't be easier

Not by afar

But at least you can watch it

Perched on a star

Then you will see all the other souls

Try to shimmer as well

Overcome obstacles

Their own private hell

Send them a lifeline

What else can you do

You love so very deeply

That's what you do.

11/10/15

Omniscience

Toss your atoms in the ether
Catch them on the wind
Scatter them beyond all reason
Where time and space begin

Throw your voice into the sky
To worlds beyond the night
Follow it to that ageless place
Where your true self first took flight

Twirl and revel in your joy
Dance partner with a star
Realize the personified love
That you really are.
4/29/14

The Coat That You Wear

Power tried to pull love down
By hanging on its coat
Love took off the garb it didn't need
That pulled upon its throat

Power put on the jacket
It pretended to be good
Everyone hung on its every word
As power hoped they would

Power made a factory
To mass produce the coats
All strutted around and puffed themselves up
Which added to their bloat

After a while, they looked around
Realized they had been had
With everyone pretending to be love
Left all in power feeling bad

With everyone drunk with power
The bar had been lowered to the floor
There was just a petty existence
Love wasn't around any more

Everyone now wore power suits
It had become the trend
No one remembered how to be themselves
They had thread bare coats to mend

Until a few brave adventurous souls
Peeled their overcoats off
They dreaded more a loveless life
Than how society would scoff

They realized immediately
How their coat had weighed them down
Now they had their freedom
They floated off the ground

The moral of the story is
If you are feeling in despair
It isn't because you aren't worthy of love
It may be the coat you wear.

Integrity's Blueprint

Give more than you get
Reap less than you sow
Listen more than you speak
Realize more than you know

Calm much more than agitate
Question more than comply
Hold yourself to higher standards
Extinguish every lie

Dream bigger than attainable
Realize your own worth
Create thoughts of originality
Celebrate every birth

Lead when there needs leadership
Follow when it seems best
Acknowledge greatness in us all
Ignore everything that's left

Have a higher calling
Know a greater truth
Have the wisdom of experience
Flexibility of youth

Cheer the world to victory
If only in your mind
Make changes you envision
Forgive those running blind

Follow your inner compass
Do everything you can
To uplift the course of humanity
By loving the heart of man

12/17/14

Humanity

When did I become invisible
Unable to be seen
When was the last time I caught a glimpse of myself
Without feeling so unclean

When was the last time my heart didn't feel shame
For merely being undressed
When was the last time I laid down my head
Without feeling so much unrest

I Am Humanity personified
I gently walk amongst the crowd
Continuously striving to bring everyone to Love
Merely by voicing out loud

I work every day to perpetuate kindness

Encourage others to do their best

I stand wincing against a wave of resistance

Waiting for indifference to crest

When there is someone starving in the world

I feel their hunger pangs, too

When you have laid crying alone in your bed

I've laid with you and cried with you, too

How did so many forget their dreams

Or, how to listen to their intuition

When did this great experience of life

Become one big institution

Why did so many forget all their dreams

Or, how to manifest them into form

When did kindness, forgiveness and truth

Become the exception and not the norm

I now realize when I became invisible

As silly as it may seem

We all lost sight of Humanity

When we lost the ability to dream.

10/13/14

GMOs

Hell No! I won't go
Don't turn me into a GMO

All this worry just tears me apart
I want to keep my human heart

Please don't make my skin out of rubber
I'd cry saline tears when I blubber

Please don't give me silicon eyes
That are kept in boxes in medical supplies

First it was veggies, now it is trees
Soon they'll be making mechanical bees

I don't want to evolve into a drone
I want progress and science to leave me alone

The world should be left organic and green
I echo the cry of voices unseen

Every living organism wants to remain real
Think of the inhumanity. How would you feel

If all of your gifts, your intangible wealth
Was removed so you'd last longer on a shelf

If our essence, our nature was stripped clear away
So we'd look better when we were put on display

Everything we do to others could happen to us
If those who know better don't put up a fuss

It's against our nature to have to disagree
But it is for nature itself that we make this plea...

Stop this human ignorance that thinks only of self
Or someday it will be humans who are kept on a shelf.
10/24/14

Give a Life Its Due

When does life begin
Who am I to say
Who and what's important
To put it another way

To defend the human zygote
Protect it to extremes
But disregard the plight of children everywhere
Is hypocrisy, it seems

How about quality of life
People get up in arms
But when a precious child is born
Who ensures that it doesn't starve

What if it's from a different race or creed
Or from a different land
Is it treated with the same regard
As a generic fetus can command

Why does it seem so much better
To be born with skin that's white
Does this genetic propensity
Better assist a world in plight

These are the questions I struggle with
In an unsettled part of me
How can one claim to wholeheartedly love God
Yet happily cut down a tree

Why do so many still hate and judge
And think that it's okay
To control those who are different
In the name of the God of the day

Why are guns so prevalent
Why is it a sacred right to shoot
But when one speaks of the right NOT to be shot
The point is dismissed as moot

Why do my sincere questions
Fall on such deaf ear
Why are so many indignant about God
Yet, with their actions, show they don't care

I've accumulated questions
From current events through the years
Like, what is the conversion of the closing Dow
Into human tears

I will continue to ask the questions
Not caring what others may think
Maybe it'll help someone somehow
By committing these musings to ink

There's a reason why so many are scared
To let their views be heard
The infinite way man defiles himself
Is literally absurd

Yet, if the quality of a single life
Can benefit from a point of view
Then I will happily do what I can
To give that life its due.

11/28/14

Flashpoint

How do you know that

The next altruistic act

Serendipitous encounter

Grandiose epiphany

Rant

Cry

Struggle

Simple act of kindness

Quiet resolve

Sincere smile

Honest self-reflection

Is not the flashpoint

That uplifts all of Humanity

With its purity of intent

And alignment to the moment?

One Note

I am a new person each moment
The one I am at the core
I am more free, lighter and happier
Than I was just a moment before

I can sing my own praises
I can dance in the mist or the rain
I can embrace every tragedy
As it teaches me to let go of the pain

I can actually swim with the fishes
Even if it's in my own mind
I commune with the dolphins, whales and the seals
As I leave all illusion behind

I continuously consult with my mentors
The long-standing wisdom of trees
They tell me the truth that men no longer speak
They send it to me on the breeze

I can withstand almost anything
Loss, loneliness, the plight of our youth
But I can't wear the lies of this world
I no longer will bury my truth

Which is...

You are a mystery waiting to reveal
You are the answer you seek
Open yourself up and just look inside
Whatever you tell you, just speak

Sing it to all who will listen
Knowing much will fall on a deaf ear
But it is so worth the performance
If even one note reaches someone to hear
3/28/16

Balance

I am a windfall
I am a tree
I am everything that comes
So sweetly to be

I am a rainfall
I am a drought
I dry up all adversity
Then pour myself out

I am the wild fires
Burning out of control
They indeed have a purpose
They too have a role

I burn up negativity
Then chill myself out
I am the fire hose
I put myself out

I am every child
Who is fleeing from war
Their life has a purpose
And more to explore

I am the soldier
Who wraps them in wire
The fear in their heart
Caused by political mire

I am the calm
When one is laid to their rest
Know they've given their all
And just did their best.
9/15/15

What Happens When

When you give your approval to something you don't agree with
You are diminishing your own voice
When you agree to a negative statement
You are lowering your vibrations
When you comply just to keep peace
You give away your power
When you appease
You are empowering someone else
When you say something you don't mean
You are dissipating your credibility

When you make a promise that you don't keep

You are splitting your energy into two streams:

The one you walk and the one you agreed to walk

When you believe in something without question

You are giving away your ability to discern

When you follow out of fear

You live in fear

When you preach without the answers

You preach ignorance

When people blindly lead

You have blind followers

When you find fault

You are showing yours (faults)

When you show indifference

You create a wound

When you ignore

You create a ghost

When you dismiss anyone as unimportant

You just missed an opportunity to truly know your own depth

6/7/14

Permission

There's nowhere to go
Nothing to do
No one to please
This day is for you

Nothing to conquer
Nothing to lose
This life is your oyster
It's yours to peruse

Freedom is yours
No need to ask why
Just put up your feet
And give it a try.

The Shift

In past lives…
We were called out for speaking our mind,
Tortured for being strong willed,
Deemed a criminal for being literate,
Sacrificed for being pure,
Treated like property for being beautiful,
Pitted against each other for being strong,
Excommunicated for communing with God,
Called a heathen for communing with nature,
Called lazy or flaky for wanting peace,
Shot for desertion for running from war,
Put into slavery for the color of our skin,
Demoralized for whom we loved,
Preached to that money was evil,
Born to people who hate us....

No wonder people have cringed within a corner of their own energy field and are afraid of their own empowerment.

It is time to...
Be beautifully bold,
Speak our truth,
Value wisdom,
Pull away from the pack,
Give homage to the God of one's choosing, the one that empowers them to love,
Love in a rainbow of diversity,
Embrace freedom,
See the cleanliness of being filthy rich,
Reject conformity,
Unfurl one's wings,
Dance on a whim,

Speak one's heart,
Honor the greatness in each other,
Empower all,
Strip the illusion off the power mongers,
Walk all over their puny insignificance,
Take our power back,
Redistribute power to the individuals who are still scratching their head,
Enliven hope,
Enliven wonder,
Enliven the world,
Hug a forest!
Be vulnerable,
Express virtue,
Speak of love,
Be demonstrative in loving life,
Live our purpose,
Share our dreams,
Nurture kindness,
Teach in a million ways,
Speak in a million tongues,
Re-adopt a simpler lifestyle,
See beauty in its true form,
Forgo dis-ease,
Uplift consciousness,
Awaken in the spirit of Love!

Daily Checklist

Wake up grateful

Remember your dreams

Record the wisdom you collected in the night

Listen to what your innate wisdom is telling you

Nurture yourself with kindness and self-care

Greet all the other souls in your home with enthusiasm

Plan an adventure for the day

Set out an intention to do something fulfilling

Validate others who serve you in the community

Acknowledge and accept all gifts graciously

Give care and nurture those who depend on you for their sustenance

Realize all the synchronicity, synergy, and flat out miracles that make your life wonderful

Be a blessing to others and yourself

Challenge others' limitations

Awaken a dream

Rekindle a spirit

Motivate the masses

Uplift humanity

Empower a world

Expound on a vision

Stretch your capacity to love

Accept all that you give in the natural ebb and flow of expansion

Awaken to your guides

Embrace all your teachers

Accept all your lessons

Forgive your own learning curve

Let go of all interactions

Lay down your guard

Rest your head in gratitude and surrender

Awaken in your higher awareness

Surrender to the incredible wonderment of the universe.

One Little Human

One little human
Falling away from the pack
Can restore hope to the world
Bring humanity back

One little human
Stepping away from the crowd
Can feel the anguish of the multitudes
And voice it out loud

One little human
Scarred and nearly broken
Can take faith, hope, and love
Where it's never been spoken

One little human
Abiding by love's creed
Can heal the planet
Let's wish it Godspeed

One little human
It may very well be you
Can teach all other humans
What they are able to do.

Be!

Be the light that you are
Be sunshine
Iridescent, incandescent, florescent
Glow
Illuminate, emanate, transfigure
Be liquid love
Be music
Be your favorite music
Dance in your heart
Feel it in your bones
Show spontaneous kindness
Widen your horizons
Inspire others to their greatness
Invite others to dance with you
Turn up the volume on you
Live your purpose!
Set a fire under your dreams
Spontaneously combust with excitement
Be organic
Be real
Laugh at your shortcomings
Celebrate your flaws
Be perfectly imperfect!

Insignificance

News and current events are tiny flecks in a sunbeam
Wait for them to settle and dust them away
There's no need to swirl them around and breathe them in

Let no flies bite
Pay no homage to problems
The raised skin will itch for a moment, but then recede

Make no mountains out of grains of half-truths
That others want to climb and stake a claim
Or forge a path to the top to pay homage to you

Be raw and pure and unbroken and undiluted
Wash moment to moment in the sanctity of your pooled greatness
Let others drink of your integrity

Let them harmonize with you in the song of untainted grace
Awaken the starkness of ignorance
Blow the lid off indifference
Lift the prohibition on truth
Defy the status quo

Raise the bar!
Break through glass ceilings
Illuminate the heart center
Lead from love

Disarm the mechanical mind
Be spontaneously combustible with enthusiasm
A breakout voice in a choir of angels
You are a celestial song!

Resound and reverberate with the bliss of perpetual beauty
Look to no one to sustain your orbit
Expect nothing from the other stars...
...except to share the sky

Keep your dreams contained in your own rotational pull
Lest they be drawn into another galaxy

Know that when your send out your intentions to the other side
of the moon
They will circle back and meet you eye to eye
And reflect your awesomeness back to you.

The Neglected

Intentions are like whispering children
We secretly nurture our favorites
The ones that reflect our comely facade
The ones that carry a testament to our greatness

Those that were nursed out of obligation and weaned by ripping
them off the teat
We sling them with venom to the farthest outreach of our
desires
And watch glazed eyes as they splatter on the wall
Dripping out life force as they slide down

Those that were clung to too strongly
Suckle still on complacency within the hidden walls of our
disdain
And die a prolonged death...
Poisoned by an implosion of their own want

The neglected
Miraculously escape scrutiny
Are spewed out like in a sneeze during the changing of the guard
These are the ones that are picked up by the wind
And germinate in a field of a new era.

Being Real

To belong to anything is to be owned
To be owned is to be enslaved
An unwitting dupe in the Ponzi schemes of society
Ah...of society itself

Be the victimless loner who's done their time
Learned their lessons, strewn their gifts
Dusted and harvested their own crop
Made a home from prefabricated boards of resilience

Compassion and contentment are your currency
Let go of the false sense of entitlement that suffering eludes to
Be contained within a sovereign state amongst the masses
Remain defenseless and unwitting with no claim on
righteousness
Point no fingers!

Be a bleached blotch of purity on the fabric of humanity
Be a spot of stillness that others use as a gauge
Anchor that stillness deep into the riverbed
Be unwavering as the chaotic stream of life passes by

Hold your stance
This is what it is to be free
This is what it is to be real.

Be...

Restless in your own bliss
Brimmed to the top and spilling over
A muse of the self
Content with your own friendship
A dancing sprite impervious to the annoyance of others.

Be You!

Pointless

There is no reason to call others on their truth...
To inflict your reality on them
To do so is to impose your sense of value...
To draw your lines in their sand...
To kick over their castle
To be ego instead of love.

Judgment

When one leads with judgment
One is met with judgment
Creating a standoff

To forgo carbuncles of opinions
Creates a doorway of receptivity
The opportunity to meet as neighbors.

Playing It Safe

Dream stained pillows of lost intentions
Cover
The thin brown wrapped..."what could have beens"

Crumpled hopes and good intentions
Collect dust
In a corner on the floor

To hide our greatness is the crime
All punishment self-inflicted
Doing life with no parole
For opportunity wasted.

Live Life Boldly!

Gazelles don't go down without a fight
Stars don't just hover in the night
Dreams aren't dreamt to be suspended
Live life boldly!
As intended.

Don't Settle!

You are no one's plan B
You are not a summer replacement
Or the second harvest
A Hail Mary pass, plan B, last pick at dodge ball, a side of rice
You are not a last ditch effort!

You are center stage
The favorite Kardashian
The penthouse view
Real whipped cream on fresh brewed latte
Organic, grass fed, Grade A awesome!

You are you!

As Is

Quit keeping yourself in a jar on a shelf and expecting life to pull off your wings.

Don't keep your inner child bound and gagged in the back of a trunk.

Stop vacillating between a scorched and angry earth of another dimension and a God praising Utopia where purity reigns.

Cleanse yourself in a new perspective where a tantrum is known as manipulation and power doesn't play.

Acceptance and rejection are different sides of the same coin. Release it from your sweaty grip. You can't buy your future with it...or thrive on handouts from others.

Quit putting off living until something gives.

Splash in the pool of your own splendor. Let the world turn as it will.

Live in the tranquility of "As Is."

Friends

Friends are like ships
Each intended to sail independently
Yet too many take on water and are being towed
And too many are used as a barge
Both extremes become habit
Too many look to be towed
They call "friend" to all
Too many fall into submission
And cringe from true friendship
Sail unhindered spontaneous
Free to engage all.

Mastery

Making a left turn without help of a light
Gaining ownership of your second sight
Thriving beyond any disease
Encouraging creativity to do as it please
Walking a tight wire without the use of a net
Living and loving without one regret
Finding adventure behind every door
Being your best then ten percent more.

Friendship Defined

Friendships are not chains that we wrap around our wrist
That lock us in obligation
They are not thumbtacked "shoulds" on our chest
Or sticky note "expectations" on our sleeve

Friendships are gasps of snow-capped air
Dancing over the tree tops
That we inhale for a while
Until the exchange is complete
Then expressed into the ether
Friendships breathe, grow, expand, and thrive
Never are they sinkholes
Or weighted anchors in the river of life

Some claim amnesty by invoking the word friend
Through a hollow shell that leaves an aching in the heart
Bless these ones for time served
Before paralysis sets in

Send them dancing away like sprites before dawn
With the exhilaration of a firefly released from a jar
Free them to thrive or sleep in the light of a new day...
Whichever they prefer.

Experience

The deep, dark abyss between reality and truth
The cynical scrutiny of the decrepit to youth
The mucus-thin sheath between real and illusion
An amniotic connection between pain, joy, and their fusion

An ill-equipped father
An adept old sage
Both play their parts handsomely
On life's Shakespearean stage

Insights accrue through many lifetimes
Or can be a flash in the pan
Lightning can't strike twice
But maybe wisdom can

Again and again
We meet death as our fate
Carry over our lessons
To another embryonic state

Ignorance or bliss
Can repeat verse for verse
Life can be a series of blessings
Or a perpetual curse

One key factor
That rings as clear as a bell

We make our own heaven
Or live our own hell.

Living in Zen

Don't need to stay
Don't feel like going
Original ideas
Perpetually flowing

No judgment here
No points to belabor
Every moment of peace
Is one to be savored

Nothing to prove
No one to belittle
The world is aligned
By staying in the middle

Each soul met
Is great amongst men
Honor their presence
By living in Zen.

Your Average Best Friend

Very independent
But doesn't like to be alone
Loves a big family
Just not her own

Enjoys the beach
But doesn't like to swim
Loves to compete
But doesn't care if she wins

Loves every holiday
Is comfortable in a crowd
Every thought she thinks
She says it out loud

Prefers diner food
To five-star cuisine
Tries every diet
In her Oprah magazine

Never outclassed
Always in style
She's a signature martini
Topped off with a smile.

Qualities

On the path of life that never ends
There are forgotten byways, thankless bends
But as I learned to resonate with Hu
Life sent me a special friend in you

You are not a lover or mere friend to me
More like a brother of life, maybe
And while the gifts of spirit are all around
I thank God for the blessing of you that I've found

To give, to know, to love, and just be
And sometimes to see something special in me
Why am I blessed with a friend like you
Is a question to an answer I already knew

So as we continue to love as we do
Here is my custom fit intention for you

May you always share laughter and joy from your heart
May the love you've accrued from your life never part
To tackle every dream that you'll ever pursue
That boys all over the world be men equal to you

May the inner sounds be sweet, the outer be soft
May the lights from the heavens shine brightly aloft
May all of the greatness you are reflecting so clear
Be a fraction of what you see in the mirror

And as we stand in the heavens as pillars of light
Fragrant in God serving all in delight
After light years and light years, forever and beyond
I'll still hold so dearly the qualities that you've donned.

Individuality

A grain of sand on the shore that catches the light
That one grounded bird that learns to take flight
The unencumbered soul that unfurls to be free
That voice in dissension that learns to agree
The infant who remembers what it's like to be old
A flame that never forgets what it's like to be cold
Defeating lost hope by saying, "I can"
An experience being comfortable being woman or man
Creating a symphony one note at a time
Knowing peace during chaos, albeit sublime
The sliver of knowledge that turns into a wedge
Being pushed past all reason and jumping over the ledge
There's no separation between the foam and the sea
Illusion's the only distinction between you and what's me.

Freedom

A girl smiled at everyone
They smiled back
All was well
Then someone didn't smile back
She felt rejection
She tried harder now to please
She experienced want
Fewer people smiled
She worked harder to win them over
She learned manipulation
She came out of her center
Others stopped smiling
She felt defeated
She stopped smiling
Then stopped caring
She surrendered
Someone smiled at her
She chose not to smile back
She knew freedom.

Commitment to Me

Life itself is built on a lie
If you're born you win
You lose when you die

It's more of a continuous cycle to me
I ebb, I flow, I win, I concede

I wax, I wane, I rise, I fall
I'm both summer and winter, both infinite and small
I'm everything to everyone, yet nothing at all

I'm one grain of sand, or one massive sea
I can heal the whole planet
But what happens to me?

I disappear in the love I give out to the world
A lost, starving child
A penniless girl

With the kindness of strangers the pattern must end
Love is the whole spectrum
Not just a means to an end

It's not giving to others yet holding love at bay
Or sidestepping kindness
As I give it away

It's not putting off happiness one moment or a day
But embracing life now
In the spirit of play

It's stirring the myriad of what I'll allow
Having the richness of living
Complete me somehow

The details are fuzzy on how this can be
Yet I know it begins
With a commitment to me.

What If...

Nobody listened to you or even acknowledged you had feelings?

What if every time you got excited, someone told you to shut up or lay down?

What if you were cold, but no one cared?

What if you were tied up away from those you love just out of reach?

What if you always had to lie on the cold, hard floor and be okay with it?

What if you had to hold your bladder until someone told you to go?

What if you were taken from your family, and it was assumed you were okay with that?

What if you were not included with the family but expected to be okay with that?

What if you were sent away if you didn't meet the expectations of your family?

What if you were put to death just because you weren't cute or happy enough to make someone love you?

What if you had to rely on others for your quality of life?

How would you make out?

How would you like being a pet?

My Intention for You Is That You Know...

How dynamic you are!

All the issues that make you feel isolated are similar to how everyone else feels, so in that isolation, you are like everyone else.

Troubles aren't the end of the journey but the beginning of breaking through to the love.

Being inundated with issues is Spirituality 101 in the classroom of life.

We aren't here to succeed in the eyes of others but to gain quiet victories for ourselves.

We are our own best cheerleaders.

Feeling unworthy and diminishing yourself is so overrated.

Humility, in the sense that we have been taught, is false humility.

Life is a game of survivor and no one can vote you out but you.

You are loved beyond compare, simply by the fact that you exist.

That person who annoys you the most is a beautiful reflection of you.

We are in this together, we are connected by the love!

Indeed, we are love itself!

Traveling Light

Marauding glances
Aimlessly meandering
Laden with slumber and strife
Torn between turning over in a warm bed and the excitement of
awakening
Amongst a stream of the masses
Some walk bent, so laden with parcels
Begging others to admire their wares...
Or carry them as if they were their own
Many faces hidden behind a tower of packages
Secured from a base of overstretched arms
Too focused on each step of walking blind
While keeping up the illusion of control

A few stroll consciously
Catching smiles
Like random reflections of light
A willing synapse
Passing love through a weary pathway
Reminding others what free hands look like
What open hearts feel like
Delighting in strewn boxes
Celebrating freedom
Traveling light.

Every Time We...

Truly listen to another person

Listen to that inner voice of our internal adviser

Forgo the gossip

Turn off the TV

Play ball with our child

Take that extra walk with our pet

Take in nature

Pay attention to our dreams

Listen with our hearts

Forgo judgment

Appreciate beauty

Let someone ahead of us

See the good in others

Lead the way

Graciously follow

See the good in the world

Take notice

Show appreciation

Hold our tongue

Do without being asked

Allow someone else to shine

Put our egos in check

Take the higher ground

Give a hand up

Administer tough love

Allow someone their freedom of choice

Say a silent thank you

Give a gift from the heart
Treat others as equals
See the greatness in others
Demonstrate the greatness in ourselves
Validate another
Acknowledge the world as a whole
Put a mute button on the trash talk
Speak to angels
Pay our way
Adopt a pet
Hug someone in pain
Heal a wound
Capture a moment
Cheer someone on
Live our purpose
Manifest a reality
Create an option
Exude confidence
Accept a compliment
Connect from the heart....

We are uplifting consciousness and connecting with the heart of all!

What Society Thinks Is...

Real, is facade
Truth, is lies
Medicine, is poison
Success, is enslavement
Beauty, is illusion
Strength, is abuse
Food, is an addiction
Education, is programming

What society thinks of me, is irrelevant.

Resolve

Your heartbeat is a commitment to live
Your sweat is a willingness to try
Your dreams are you casting your intentions across the universe
Life, as you express it, is the drag
Breath is the willingness to take in all the gifts offered
Resolve is holding a cosmic place in the moment of now.

Smile

Smile like you are melting dark clouds with your kindness

Sing as if your song is your pulpit and with it you are helping others find their way

Dance as if you command the atoms around you to dance with you

Send them out to entice others to awaken to their joy

Speak as if the reverence of the universe is leaning in to listen because it is

Dream as if you open up the heart of humanity with your intention

Hug as if you are drawing in all the children of the world

To partake of their own innate innocence

Love with such tenderness that it leaves you vulnerable and exposed

Forgive all as if you are pardoning a saint

Set your inner compass by such a tender place that tears well up even at its broach

See yourself as I see you: a smoldering ember of divine love ready to set humanity ablaze with Inspiration.

Encouragement

They said you'd never amount to much
They said your dreams were out of touch
They said the "you," you want to be
Doesn't quite fit in society

They said the pain and wounded pride
Will help you take it all in stride
"It's okay to have a broken heart
But don't let them see you fall apart."

You ask,
"Isn't it better if I try?"
"No! You'll be a success
When you see pigs fly."

Well there's something you need to know
Dreams, like seeds, are meant to grow
When they are put in the ground
It's only to spread their bloom around

Every dream that's deprived of air
"Possibility" hears, "I don't care."
Every "hope" that wanders in the woods
Was led astray by a trail of "should's"

For every forsaken "potential" crying
There's a wistful grounded winged pig sighing

Some may stand by and watch dreams die
But I'll be coaching the pigs to fly.

Artistry

My life is the canvas
On which I paint my truth
Wisdom intervened for me
From spilling my paint in youth

Inspiration is the well
In which I dip my pen
I'm commissioned by the gods
Yet judged in turn by men

The canvas may crack and dry
The lessons long ferment
But the artist stands by her work
Not one stroke do I regret.

Incarnating

Incarnating is how musical light beings descend
A mosaic arrangement of when light and sound blend
A delicate instrument dancing in flesh
Joy and love mix with pain in a temporal mesh

Their voice is the song of their limited decree
Of all they believe and to what they'll agree
Their eyes see through a filter of limited light
Focused on what they believe to be right

Their hands meld and transform things
In a limited lot
The Painter, the Healer
What's possible, what's not

Ears carve out a ventral
Of limited scope
That puts less into knowing
And more into hope

Their legs track the land
With the stubbornest of will
Only a relentless regard
Of what they wish to fulfill

Until the whole process
Is put back into the ground

And Soul agrees once again
To be physically bound.

When

Not if...when
Not maybe...when
Not hopefully...when

When we have world peace
When we value kindness beyond monetary gain
When we all are Joyful, Loving, Abundant and Free.

Gaining Spiritual Maturity

Oh sweet tender Soul

So terrified that you'll be plucked out of your haven

And assimilated into a nothingness

That you wrap yourself in a heavy layer of camouflage and don an identity

Pull an ego over yourself

Reinforce it with a blanket of contempt

And stuff the lining with anger and judgment

You guard yourself further with a prickly elusiveness

Smeared with excuses

Stick labels all over it: victim, weak, hopeless

Oh sweet Soul the harshness is too much to bare

So you try to lighten it with denial

Dip it in layers of feelings that mimic the tenderness of your core

These feelings actually believe the ploy, they believe they are you

Sweet Soul is overtaken by feelings and believes it is one and the same

Yet emotions are merely a tool to mimic Soul's sweetness

You slip into a shell of a coarse body of skin to further alienate your true self

Embellishing the illusion with pretty skin or a thick pocket

But you, sweet Soul, suffocate inside

You eventually cry out to be freed

The universe sweeps in to save you

Harsh experiences rip through the layers that have made you despondent

Pull you free

The skin may bleed

The feelings cry out in anguish

The mind scrutinizes, debates, and threatens insanity

The layers suffer as they are stripped away

But the sweet Soul at the core...

...The pure atoms of awareness

Rejoice at the wisdom you have accrued

The freedom that has been realized

Unfurl your greatness and settle in to your own omniscience.

Book of Life

Take a bow to things you fear
That have captured your attention
They have put a face upon
What's too hideous to mention

Past life memories buried deep
Incest, torture, murder, rage
They are teachers perhaps mentors
Dog-eared chapters in your page

Insert your page amongst the others
Take a bow to their strife
Use your love as the glue
To secure yourself in the Book of Life.

Bless This Day

Bless this day
And those I serve
May all know the truth
They so richly deserve

May all open their hearts,
Their souls, and their minds
Give others the fortitude
To truly be kind

May all open their awareness
So they can happily refrain
From abusing others
And bringing disdain

Give all the insight
So they can all see
Everyone beautifully abundant
Loving and free.

The Awakened

Truth withdrew into the mist
As ignorance blew its one last kiss
Many receded with the tide
To wait for power to subside

A few stood strong in soul's dark night
To help the wounded retake flight
They stood with backs against the wind
Waiting for the darkness to rescind

Control is the boil on power's decree
Brokers and pawns vestige their one last plea
Fear, anger, jealousy are their stance
To manipulate who leads in the final dance

Many awaken in the final round
Many more warriors start to rebound
Those that were fractured beyond compare
Spontaneously heal and start to repair

The wind is mild, the current is right
For the multitudes to take flight
They pull away from power's last try
Join the legion of awakened into the sky.

A Satisfied Life

When is the last time you:

Fell into bed exhausted
Got drunk on laughter
Was terrified your heart was going to burst out of your chest
Gave your word and kept it
Took a chance
Made love in nature
Made love to nature
Made love to yourself
Got soaking wet in your good clothes
Tackled your own demons, slapped them on the back, and took
them out for a drink
Challenged authority to a fist fight
Kicked the teeth out of conformity
Got so dirty that you crunched grit
Did anything to your heart's content
Manifested a dream
Changed the world for the better
Loved unconventionally
Thought an original thought

Life is about getting dirty, cleaning up, breaking down, building
back up,
Thriving,
Growing,
Changing,

Adapting,

Leaving everything that you are...mingled in the dust, the clouds, and the puddles

And being greater for your own decomposition and reconstruction.

The Empowerment of Words

Words can be daggers

Or they can be a balm to a weary soul

They can be blueprints to a mansion

Or a bulldozer to raze dreams to the ground

They can hold space for beauty, integrity, and kindness

Or they can create a purgatory or hell that is hard to emerge from

They can give encouragement and kindness

Or rip away all hope

We are master craftsmen with our words

Smiths of an indelible bounty

We choose

Whether in conscious awareness

Or in ignorance by default

We are the empowered

Always the empowered.

Yet

When you've given all you can
But choose to go another round
When you've had the snot kicked out
Yet stand and hold your ground

When your wings have been crushed
For "who knows why"
Yet you manage to navigate
And find a way to fly

When you are totally dismissed
And left without a voice
But manage somehow to get heard
You simply have no choice

When everyone seems to lie
Denying their highest truth
Yet you hold all accountable
From world leaders to the youth

When your heart has been a battlefield
A perpetual "push turns to shove"
Yet you manage to transcend it all
And find a way to love

When you pour yourself into all you do
With nothing else to give

Then you have found the answer you seek
On "What's the proper way to live?"

Life

Life is not a competitive sport
There's no need for commentaries
No first prize
No best in show
No elimination round
No judgment
No official uniform
No rulebook
It's not a betting sport
Not pass/fail
No win by default
Everyone's a winner
No one's in the dugout shaking their head if you strike out
Life is a win-win scenario
You show up, you win
It is a classroom
Everything's a lesson
Everyone has potential
Everyone gets a prize
Existing is the prize
Being able to wake up
Arrange each day

Plant a seed

Perpetuate an intention

Love something

Love anything

Choose, decide, question

Thrive, evoke, elicit

Dream, imagine, create

Inspire, conquer, empower

Kick in that sand castle

Build it again

As many times as you desire

As many times as it holds interest

As many times as there is one iota of learning from doing so

Again and again

No judgment, no error

Just you with your joy and desire

And love

Learning and being...

On the perpetual shores of love.

Ignite

Share in others' joy
Their joy is your joy as well
Honor truth everywhere
Truth is home
See beauty in others
It enhances your own (beauty)
Revel in the abundance of life
Want and need are an illusion
See freedom for all
To see otherwise is enslavement
Perpetually love
To stay afloat on a river of love and compassion
Honor all beings
To empathize
Is to pull the dagger out of your own long forgotten wound
Breathe life into all embers
To ignite a world
One breath at a time
One moment at a time
One realization at a time.

Search and Rescue

I delve into a pool of quiet conviction
Emerge in a sweat soaked sheet of despair
Believing you have left me somehow
As I reach for you and find nothing there

Sounds have become tinny and off key
Vision has been blurred through the tears
I am dimwitted and dumbfound
To feel that my God doesn't care

I have fought for you through many lifetimes
Ruthlessly defended your stance
Shamelessly praised you until my voice was left raw
But can't even feel you in any romance

All of the victory claims
All of the conjecturing from within
All of the pompous deflecting
Went the way of my original sin

Each kindness is now a sweet victory
From foolish brash hearted pride
It is in emptying myself of all else
That I can feel you welling inside

Now I understand your true nature
It is as pure as a hint of the wind

It is the stillness now that embraces me
Causing all subtle doubt to rescind

You are the Light, the Love and the Music
You are the curve of my smile
I searched for you with every advantage
You sat with me all of the while

Now I know how to serve you
By greeting you in all that I meet
No longer is ego my barometer
It's been the victor in every defeat

"Sir, Let me walk with you sweetly
Let me carry your ware"
By lightening the load of another
I will always feel God everywhere

3/20/17

More Than Family

Listen close
And you will "hear"
Constant reassurance
A sympathetic ear

A lick of the face
In agreement I suppose
The surprising delight
In an ice cold nose

The wag of a tail
The warm spot in your bed
The unbridled acceptance
From that tail to the head

Toenails that tap
As paws scamper on the floor
They are not here to obey
They are here to adore

They are closer than family
We chose them from the start
They are more than a friend
They are an extension of our heart.

We Are Humanity

We are the skin of humanity
Grace is our natural cadence
As palpable as our breath
With fluid locks of fortitude
Falling around our shoulders
And sometimes bound tightly in a decree
Drops of kindness
Beading from within
To pool at the surface
Cooling the fervor of an ominous heat
The ashen soot of outer oppression

We are elastic and resilient to stretch between the seas
And speak to the minds that have been closed
by the warfare of human want
Our heart beats in harmony with them
Our chests rise and fall in unison with them

We cry our selfish tears as we absorb the excess pain of the
unnecessary oppression of our brethren
Filling our minds and bodies with anything to dull the
foreboding
Self medicating from the insanity that is self inflicted
To deafen the anguish from within

We are the voice of humanity
Too terrified to speak our truth
Primal memories of being called out, scorned and banished

Still inhibiting the song of unison we so desperately wish to sing

Like calling birds on adjacent branches
Making sure all is well in their world
We are the songbird, the lioness and the sky
All existing with little reference point for each other
Only reaching out for ourselves in others through the familiar
depth of the calm and the respite from pain

We are both the total sum and a tiny fraction of humanity
Each one playing our part from the vantage point we are given
As important as the best
and as insignificant as the least
Registering each transgression and affliction on a random score
sheet

Cultivating the courage, strength, dignity and diligence to forge
on
Stretching the boundaries of our own worth
Expanding the consciousness of our awareness of self
Until that point where we happily and with no adulteration
Spill into each other with the spontaneous jubilation
of youth, innocence, wisdom and wonder

We are humanity
As ancient as the cosmic sea and as innocent as our last birth
Let us nurture the tenderness within us with our own
experienced stance
Let us wipe out all ignorance and greed with a disapproving
glance

Let us tend to the willful spoiled components of our self

With the discipline of self reflection and solitude they demand

We are humanity

In heart, in spirit, in song

Let us give up all judgment of the dissatisfied aspects of ourselves and put a vengeful God to rest

One who reflects the worst of man and wishes the rest to suffer in deference to him

Let us open all gates, crumble all walls, awaken all sleeping and recapture all that was once lost

We are not the one. We are the everyone

Let our brilliant light purge the thickest smudge on the window of our greatest vestige

Let Joy, Love, Abundance, Kindness and Freedom be our ware

For we are the troubadours of life

The dancing minstrels of infinity

Always awakening, always rolling incredible compassion into ourselves and testing the boundaries once again

We are humanity....

7/11/18

Jen Ward, RM, LMT

Speaking for the Unborn Life

I am a baby
Born into a hell
It was my life to forgo
Not a politician's to sell

I am a child
Living a lie
That all you need is to be born
And happiness will comply

I am a teenager
Struggling to fit in
There is so much pressure on me
When everything is a sin

I am an adult
Struggling to make my own way
It's like moving through molasses
For just a dollar a day

I am the victor
Who survived at all cost
Although nothing was handed to me
When all hope was lost

I am the voice of reason
Speaking for the unborn
Don't force them into arms

To live loveless and forlorn

Let them pass through
The membrane of quick sorrow
May they quickly re-land
In the hope of the morrow.

Section III: Truth

I Am Love

I am a Muslim - I continuously declare my faith through kindness to all others

I am a Jew - I have suffered dearly for my right to exist and have great resolve

I am a Christian - I strive to personify Christ consciousness

I am a Pagan - I see God in everyone and everything

I am a Buddhist - I think and discern for myself

I am an Atheist - I reject all tenets that do not resonate with my own sense of truth

I am an Agnostic - I question everything, especially what others tell me to believe

I am an Eckist - I understand that I exist because I am loved

I am a Hindu - I believe in the continuity of life greater than this physical form

I Am Love - I see the goodness in all others beyond all labels and personal convictions.

11/22/15

What Needs to Happen to Have Peace

Angels need a rest

Visions need to clear

Divides must be mended

Entitlements must be more fair

Dust needs to settle

From the antics of the men

Gardens must be planted

We must return to Zen

Wars must be unwaged

Fevers need to break

The proud and indignant

Must admit to their mistake

Woman must be valued

Of every sect and shape and kind

Perceptions must be given

To the deaf, mute, ignorant and blind

Truths must be spoken

All lies must rescind

Illusion must be stripped away

Released into the wind

Innocence must be revered

Above guile and deceit

Pay homage to individuality

And laid upon its feet

Reawaken from all slumber

That has rusted all resolve

Open up love's floodgates
Coax anguish to dissolve
Forgo all petty squabbles
In all we think, feel, say and do
Then peace will rest upon the land
And settle itself in you.

1/29/16

Discernment

I don't make a habit of asking for help
But will give it when it's truly warranted
I know the difference between the truth and a lie
And definitely know how to live it

I know that all that ever transpires
Will be up to debate or discussion
But I tune out all the mental fray
Just like an annoying percussion

I don't indulge in focusing on problems
Never give attention to an unworthy cause
I never listen to whiny complaints
Unless the perpetrator has paws

I feel every nuance between lies and the truth

And the truth is where I stand
It has had the wind knocked out of it
These days it just needs a hand

Kindness is a form of palpable truth
That can be felt by the discerning eye
It registers itself on all planes of existence
And encourages us to give it a try

We, together, are palpable truth
Connected by the Love
We are all agents of truth learning to thrive
As below, to reflect the above.

Sing

Hold a steady course
Don't give in to the mind
Not being able to see the solution
Doesn't mean you're blind

Feel into it with your heart
Perhaps into your soul
Being kind, loving and free
Is the ultimate goal

You can't get there in theory
Or on the backs of the crowd
It happens in knowing truth
And voicing it aloud

You can't arrive by squelching
The dreams of another
This isn't a human race
But a co-op sister-brother

Delve into the trenches
Hide there if you will
Love and truth are your mainstay
You will be love in there still

It doesn't matter how you distract

From the ultimate goal

No matter what you believe

You're still Love, you're whole

Look up from your drudgery

The one in which you cling

You were not meant to suffer

You were meant to sing.

Nameless One

What do I call you

Not a word that the multitudes use to curse others

Father?

My father disappointed and abandoned me

Lord?

Kings have been using that word for eons to wield power

That is not you

Holy Ghost?

This conjures up the image of lost souls

Trinity?

A trendy girl's name

All words diminish the depth of your Being

So how do I define you

With a simple spontaneous smile given and received a thousand times a day

How do I revere you

By disturbing the tranquility of your stillness as little as possible

And sharing the gifts that you have allotted me

With gratitude

May every moment be an homage to you.

Peace on Earth

When the law of the land is to see value in every individual

Not as a collective grunt to dominate

Control, enslave, imprison, desecrate, invalidate or throw away

But as awesome individuals...each a jewel to cultivate

Compressed from unique experiences

Faceted to contribute according to their abilities

Shimmering in their purpose

Each mind a plethora of knowledge

With the ability to discern and self-govern

Each heart beating in rhythm with humanity

Each being a song with a sacred quality

Always bettering ourselves generation after generation

With the ultimate goal of Life, Liberty and the Pursuit of Happiness for All

Not merely those who have been born with the right skin color, tax bracket, gender, sexual orientation, etc.

But ALL!

It is then, and only then, that we will all be endowed with

Peace on Earth.

The Only Voice That Matters

If someone...

Tells you to be quiet
It means you have something to say

Tells you to work
Respond by going to play

Says that you're ugly
They're missing your beauty within

Tells you you're bad
They are caught up in sin

Lies to your face
They are really lying to themself

Tells you how to behave
It is they that is put on a shelf

Perceives you as poor
They are demonstrating lack

Believes they are "owed"
It's proof their not giving back

Everything others convey
Is the depth of their own truth
Some stay in shallow waters
Well past their youth

It is you who need to dismiss
Everything they think, say or do
The only voice that matters
Is the one within you.
6/25/15

The Rear View Mirror

What is the point in looking backwards
What purpose does it serve
It is like driving and being fixated on the rear view mirror
When I help people, they want to talk about that ditch they were in
They are fixated on the ditch
Like it was an exciting adrenalin rush to get out of it
Or, they are amazed that they are free
So many want to go back and look at the depth of the ditch
"Ooh...look at the tread marks we left"
What they don't realize is they are driving back to the ditch
They expect me to hang around with them, fixated on the ditch
I won't drive back there with them
They want to describe what it was like to be stuck
Trust me...I know
Once you are free, it is important to keep driving
Stay focused on the journey
Your journey
Keep your eyes forward
Because Items seen in the rear view window
Are closer than they appear.

No Reason

There is no reason to call others on their truth...
To inflict your reality on them
To do so is to impose your sense of value
You are using your past experiences to dictate their future
To draw your lines in their sand
To kick over their castle
To be ego instead of Love.

Sighting

The conclave line on an inner circle
Parallel to the setting sun
Framed by the arch of myth or legend
An oblique sighting of "what could have been"

The brightest star in the farthest dimension
Waving whimsical and free
Was it in a dream or aspiration
I recognize that star as me.

True Worship

Love is my religion
Joy is my decree
Where I am standing is where I worship
My altar is "just me"

Kindness is my donation
Giving is my prayer
I don't just send it to the sky
I send it everywhere

Empowering others is my conviction
Needing nothing is my strength
Inspiring is being the wayshower
To which I do in length

My halo is invisible
My wings are folded in
I'd rather show others their own virtue
Than threaten them with sin

Seeing good in others
Is the flame I stoke
I prefer to bless them with my words
Than regret anything I ever spoke

I command the heavens
To part the clouds of night
So all can know their windfall
In Sound, in Love and Light

Join me on this journey
To the worlds of calm, so still
Where everyone is empowered
And centered in free will

There is no more point in taking
From a spiritual standpoint you'll see
That by truly giving heart, mind and soul
Is the express pass to be free.

6/15/16

The Celebration

"Anger" took one look around
He had his reasons. They all were sound

For every outcry and display
Every injustice he did relay

The price he paid was all too dear
The kingdom was too numb to hear

"Indifference" was just in this same stance
But now it was "Anger" with the ugly glance

"Pride" and "Arrogance" were forlorn
For it was "Anger" from which they're born

"Hate" stood burning their heritage
As "Love" knitted together a solid bridge

"Arrogance" took one last look around
He dropped his tilted ugly crown

"Pride" dramatically fell to his knees
Tossed "Grace" and "Kindness" the palace keys

There was a different sort of dance
Once "Grace" and the "Kindness" could relax

No longer twisted in a spire
The guests could now rise above the mire

"Joy", "Love", "Abundance" inwardly crept
From the chambers where they wept

As they were seated back where they belong
The celebration erupted in song

If you were there you'd know the score
"Pride" and "Vanity" are no more

"Truth" and "Integrity" have regained its reign
In the heart of Humanity it will remain.
11/14/16

Misnomers

Kindness is not a weakness

Opinions are not truth

Judgments are not facts

Wielding power is not strength

Showing Love is not a vulnerability

Sharing is not losing, but an exponential gain

Giving is not giving, but receiving

Taking up a cause is not transcending power; it is making it your equal

Silence is not invisible

Conversation is not a tradeoff for connecting

Society is not a reflection of humanity

Problems are not meant to be downloaded onto others

Sympathy is not compassion; Sympathy is rubbing an eternal wound

Compassion is disallowing the wound to be re-opened

The past only defines us if we bring it into the present

There is no future only consecutive moments

Religion is merely a step towards God

The heart of Love is entered beyond the mind

Higher Love is not ward and fuzzy but a deep contentedness

Complacency is a form of death

Others do not see your faults with the same magnifying glass as you

Problems are gifts to hone our spiritual strength

Beauty is a recognition of an inner Light

An enemy is the flip side of a friend

Most are not afraid to die but to be separated from their consciousness

Everyone is on a mecca to truth so there is no need to save anyone

We are not individuals but atoms in the body of Love

Love is not something to strive for but to recognize from within

Everyone is loveable; it is what they have accumulated that is not

No one is an island; one's uplifting thoughts, deed and actions uplift all

Humility is seeing your greatness but seeing that same greatness in all

The mind is not God; the mind is a computer that we defer to out of habit

Our physical body is just a vehicle to operate to gain experiences

More people are afraid of living than of dying

It is impossible to die, only to wear out our vehicles.

People are afraid to speak their truth because of persecution in past lives

Our fears already played out in past lives so we can let them go

Herd mentality plays on a primal fear of being picked off in a herd

You are now above all this.

What It Is to Be Free

I am a cavern that love pours in
The echo of sound, crisp and full
Beckons me to quench this thirst for truth
With the skill of a craftsman and the eagerness of youth

All my atoms are charged, eager and lithe
As they expand in rhythm to a greater awareness
Pulling away from the illusion of form
Like the heat of the sun dissipates the girth of a storm

In an altered state, I experience "I Am"
If I can do it, everyone can
My atoms that know that I am inevitably free
Stretch through the Universe to know all they can see

While the mind thinks it's this solid matter
Your atoms are craving permission to scatter
To stretch through the Universe as ambassadors of you
Infiltrate your illusion with what's really true

In this way, we all blend and blur
We discover the secret to how to endure
Realizing what we experience under ego's rule
Is our personal lesson plan in our own private school

In energy we are never so trapped

We go wherever our imagination can see

The only prison that there really can be

Is the mind that can't fathom what it is to be free.

3/18/15

What You Are Capable of

Can you be someone's guardian
Give from an infinite source
Can you gently guide them back on track
When they get veered off their course

Can you be a champion
Of Light, and Love, and Truth
Can you inspire the very old
'Temper the foolishness of youth

Can you wrap your love around
The mute, the deaf, the blind
Can you help them speak and hear
And see the world as kind

Can you teach the selfish
What satisfaction it is to give
Can you passionately imbue the disheartened
With a joyful conviction to live

Can you teach a random stranger
The in-depth philosophy of a tree
Can you help them, heart, soul and mind
To be completely free

Can you gather all your courage

To be loving to the core

This is what you're capable of, my friend

All this, and so much more.

9/14/14

Life's Greatest Monument

Silence is the scourge of earth
When power and selfish combine
It's all that good people think they can do
Just watch without losing their mind

They lose their voice, hold their tongue
Terrified of themselves wielding power
When will they realize to initiate their part
Instead of waiting for the final hour

Being polite, walking away
Were conditioned in us for a reason
When arrogance wears the mighty crown
Speaking truth is a grand act of treason

Caucasian is a power suit of the day
Trimmed with a brocade of moral outrage
Is God a grand player in judging the masses
Or does truth speak through the healer and sage

We all fear that trembling cadence of truth
When it finally shakes through the land
But it won't come as a volcanic eruption
For it's revealed in each grain of sand

The more we practice truth in our life
And challenge power with "why?"
The more we can crumble the spine of the bully
To cause both power and ignorance to die

Like why would God instill love in two hearts
And then somehow deem it wrong
How come those who love seem so weak
And those who hate seem so strong

Why would God make us so different
Yet expect us to worship the same?
Are people really so ignorant or stupid
To think they serve him when they kill in his name?

How does anyone gain our trust
Yet turn around and judge with such vengeance?
Is there any room in someone's dense psyche
To remove ignorance to instill a transcendence?

Am I writing as an act of indulgence
Or does anyone care about this truth?
Can anyone change their stance in midlife
Or do we have to rely again upon youth?

Is anyone out there ready to decree

That they understand that they hold the power

Not to wield it against anyone

But to keep their own life from going sour?

You are the God force contained in a body

Love is the preservative element

Truth is your bite, Joy is your charm

Your kindness is life's greatest monument.

4/7/15

Love As the Initial Cause

Ignorance is ignorance

Abusing power is abusing power

Complacency is complacency

People are people

Judging in judging

Hate is hate

Love is Universal

The same invisible hate that goads ISIL to murder

Has its foothold in America in proselytizing hate against gays

What is the difference?

Hate is hate

God is not a hater

People who think God hates are making God in their own image

The lesson in power is getting old...those of us who Love choose
a different experience

It is time for the shroud of ignorance to be cast from the eyes of
the complacent

Let each soul of love speak up just a little more in defense of
love

There is nothing noble in being meek

The meek shall inherit the earth

Those who are empowered in love will inherit all of heaven

When you speak truth in your small world, the ripple of truth ebbs out and bends the sword of power

When you are loving and kind in your day, power dries up a little bit more on the other side of the world

You are no bit player

You are just not afforded the ability to see the affect of your cause

Make love and kindness your cause and watch how quickly it takes hold in the world

Don't wait for someone else...you be the initial cause

You know you want to

You know you are able

You know how dynamic and empowered you are

Make love your impassioned pleas to all humanity

Make love be your benchmark of this life

Make love be your golden footprint

Save the world from the ruthless acts that you hold secret memories of

Take a stand

And when you fly away...

You will be carried away with your own wings of love

Reclaim Your Empowerment

You are important

You matter

All of the Universe conspires on behalf of your joy

All of life cheers you on with every little victory

It is disappointed when you reject your own empowerment

It is concerned when you are discouraged

Cries your pain in the howling of the wind

Cleanses your anger with the rushing of the raging water

Seers love into your depth through the warmth of the sun's glow

Life taps the ash off your lit end through little difficulties

All of your atoms are holding hands with all the atoms of everyone and everything else in the world

We all jump into the circle of our own wonderment together

You are a part of all

You are a golden fiber woven into an infinite thread count

Your light and sound interlaces intricately into the Universal tapestry

You are the dot on the second "i" in rejoicing

You matter

Believe

Rejoice

And reclaim your empowerment.

10/13/15

Gaia Speaks

The cold strikes the human sky
Huddled in dwellings the natives ask why

Buried in arrogance and piles of snow
Believing there's nothing they don't possibly know

As a species they desecrate all natural gifts
Indifference accumulates in heavy white drifts

Cycles of weather come and go
Indolence the only fruit man's willing to sow

So many lessons left on the table
Humanity crippled by the willing and able

"Power" let out one last haughty laugh
Willing to sacrifice the last fatted calf

It will run this world to the ground
Frack it to ashes, a lifeless mound

'Til Gaia stepped in with an even brow
To balance the scales in the "here and now"

Dispensing truth that was once called treason
Gifting many with the ability to reason

Restoring justice back to the land
As a handful stand by who understand

There's no need to hoard what's in the ground
When abundance and blessings are all around

There's no need to take an eye for an eye
Leaving a glazed over society, unable to cry

Abundance for all! The original decree
Is restored to every man, animal, species and tree

Taking for taking's sake is finally disarmed
Greed, glitz and gluttony stripped of its charm

Abusive power has become the enemy at large
As it finally sinks in, it's no longer in charge

In this ruthless weather, one stark truth ensues
The restoration of humanity exists in the empowerment of you

Thinking you are unworthy, unable to cope
Is telling everyone to give up all hope

Get off your ass...shake off the crumbs
Pound feeling back into your parts that went numb

You're not on the sidelines of some spectator sport
You are here to get messy, get involved, give support

The small "you" you thought you were was part of the lie
You can see through the illusion if you give it a try

Everyone is a super hero with their own special power
When you don't share your gifts, you just grow mean and sour

Embrace all your talents...hone all your crafts
The weather will break when you get this! Alas...

One more truth that you really need to see
Gaia speaks to your heart through this message from me.

Dear Universe...

Thank you for all the times that I have been misunderstood

It has taught me to strive to understand others

Thank you for all the times that I was invisible

It has taught me to validate those whom others have overlooked.

Thank you for all the times that I have cried

There is so much Joy in simply being tear free

Thank you for all the people that resent me

They have made me realize that it's not possible to please them so there is no need to ever waiver from my truth to try

Thank you for all the people who have rejected me

They have taught me to enjoy my own company

Thank you to all those who have let me down

They have pointed me in the direction of saving myself

Thank you for all the time I have been alone

It has taught me the language of other species, trees, and nature

Thank you for my lack of competitive spirit

It has led me to see everyone as a winner and configure every scenario as win-win

Thank you for showing me such ugliness

So I can strive a little more to see beauty everywhere

Thank you for showing me cruelty

It shows me that people are lashing out from their own suffering

Thank you for my ability to withstand pain

It is less excruciating than seeing it inflicted on someone else

Thank you for giving me just enough of each lesson that I
needed

Thank you for my capacity to love and heal and thrive and know
peace under all circumstances

Thank you for my ability to help others find their strength

Thank you for weaving me into such a beautiful expression of
compassion.

Heal All

Motives are transparent

Like concentric rings on a still pond

With one emanation intention

To the naked eye seems selfish

Notice me

Give to me

See my importance

But the compassionate looks deeper

See me

I have been ignored, abandoned, rejected, defiled

Notice me

So I no longer wander alone as an apparition

Recognize me

So that I know that I exist

Give to me

I have been starved to emaciation

Robbed of all I hold dear

Stripped to the bone

Raped and left crumpled in the dirt

Give to me so I can clothe my shame

Give to me so I can bind and balm my wounds

Give to me so I can rest on a pile of false pride

Until I can endure more of the journey to my true self

See me

See me so I can feign strength

See me so I can shake off the haughty mocking from within

See me so I can anchor myself in relationship to you

See me so I can wade through the myriad of shame that
accompanies me

Yes the compassionate eye looks past the ripples

Into the depth of the stillness of the pond

It sees pure intention that is too shy to try

Innocence that has lost its way

Truth that has gone mute

Compassion acknowledges these

Encourages pure intention

Empowers innocence

Speaks with truth in the ancient tongue of stillness

Heals a heart

Heals a land
Heals their own self inflicted wounds
Heals all.

7/7/14

Homage to You

You are as fluid as an ocean
More expansive than the sky
As determined as an echo
More breathless than a sigh

Astonishing as a windpipe dream
That meets its manifestation
As pure as the providence of soul
At its final destination

You are a joyful whisper
Completed in a smile
The perfect pair of stylish shoes
That can go the extra mile

You are divinity personified
That leaves no doubt, no less
Where alpha and omega meet
Is you, humanly expressed.

The Brilliance of Your Form

You are way too magnificent and expansive to focus all your attention on a pimple on your face.

Why do you define yourself by a little extra girth on your body?

Don't you realize that it represents all the pain and struggle and sacrifice you have endured just to exist here?

How dare you let anyone shame you?

How dare you shame yourself with silly words like fat or ugly?

Don't you realize that you are made of the same stuff as the heavens? Even the Gods?

Who cares what shoes you wear?

Who cares if your purse matches your dress?

Who made these rules?

Was it someone who has watched over your struggle through the eons and has blessed you every step of the way?

Or is it a force that shames, coerces and manipulates all the beauty of creation into conformity?

Which voice do you listen to when you lay your head down at night?

Or when you are doing your best to care for your loved ones?

Or merely trying to get through yet another cycle of the day?

Are you blessing the world with your greatness?

Or are you cursing yourself with personal admonishment?

There is no enemy coming for you.

There is no one that is making it their mission to destroy you.

That is all done by you with your petty thoughts and haunting beliefs.

It's okay to discharge that inner taskmaster...of the duty of admonishing you.

No one will rebuke you for showing kindness to yourself.

Yet all of the heavens will sing at this one act of sweet rebellion.

When you finally realize, finally understand the sacred trust you are given...to love all of life through yourself.

Then you unlock the mystery of all of life.

That you are the doorway to the infinite.

When you belittle yourself, you shut the door on the wonders of the Universe.

Awakening entails forgoing the constant barrage of the self-deprecating onslaught.

It is to be at peace with all the flecks and inflections in your perfect wonder

And revel in them as they catch and reflect the light.

As you unabashedly celebrate the brilliance of your form in dance.

11/29/16

Transcendence

Beyond godly borders on which nationality depends
Is the universal war cry for humanity to transcend

All the etchings in marble, the writings in stone
Are left to remind us—we don't do it alone

Walls are not made to keep us living in fear
They're to uphold a vision for all to hold dear

Beyond the facade of what we all know
Is good versus evil going toe to toe

The same struggle that takes place between us and our brethren
Is reflective of what's fought between our hell and our heaven

The same battle that's fought in our family and home
Is the same that played out in ancient Greece, Athens, and Rome

The same selfish desires and pettiness of plan
Is seen a billion times over in the struggle of man

When we conquer in dreams, put the ego in check
Take a moment from the drama, take time to reflect

It is clearly visible that on which we depend
Is an illusion that evaporates once we transcend.

The...

The quivering line between horizon and ocean
The magnetic play between stillness and motion
The oil of the sweat of a labor of love
The knee jerk relief when escaping a shove

Ten million moments conjoined in an hour
The disarming grace of a play without power
The biting cry of a fallen bird's call
Recovering your dignity after a fall

The rhythm created when writing a poem
The sanctity felt when journeying home.

Universal Healer

An echo fills the ancient sky, there's heard one universal cry

Percussions, movement, rhythms blend, hands that heal, bodies mend

The dance to capture visions lost, regain freedom at any cost

Broken lives we all endure, the sacred potion is the cure

To wash away the ills of man, unite us with our tribe again

In this life few understand what the Shaman can withstand

To ease the suffering of those she can, heart to heart and hand to hand

Eons later, old friends dispersed to meet as strangers is their curse

Ways of remembering now dull and gray, all searching for the easy way

The healer steps forward in the artificial light to show the brilliance of true sight

Ancestors emerge in dance within with spirits of the earth and wind

Calling forth surging powers within, her presence urges shadows to rescind

All seekers of truth squint to see the humble stance of the Shaman's decree

Light and sound blend and blur as she summons truth to re-emerge

She blows away the waves of pain to bring back love to the heart
of earth again

With the bending of the light, others come forth out of the night
Clans remember how to serve the land and their vows to reunite

We meet again across time and space, recognition in a weary
face
A fellow healer endured at all cost, and many times thought all
was lost

Feel the blessings that ensue when one lost crusader learns
there's two
Exponential healing has begun, Freedom now has been re-won.

Relax in Your Stance

Your power is not power...
But a position you hold in the universe
It is you being plugged in

To leave that stance is to
Flail in the starkness of space
Begging others to define you

To be empowered, just step back into alignment
Let go of whatever you are clutching
And relax in your own stance

You are the sun in your universe
Your aspirations are the stars
Let all navigate to and around you

Be their gravitational pull
Stay centered in your orbit for all is well
Be indifferent to asteroids of drama

Let no concern for the vastness of space
Or the stark illusion of the night
Disturb your embers

Be the omniscience that you seek

Be the omnipresence that you sense
Be the omnipotence that you are.

Words

"Hope" is a flickering barge drifting off in the night sky

"Knowing" is comfortably sleeping in its crow's nest

"Wanting" is grasping for a trinket a feather's length away

"Having" is clutching it in your fist

"Maybes" are musing fits of wistfulness

"Shoulds" are reprimands thrown at others

"Contentment" is the down-covered shoulds, wants, and maybes sleeping under protective wing.

The Land of Empowerment

Surrender is not giving up
But severing the allegiance to the ego
The perpetrator of all war crimes
With its iron-clad blue prints into the reckless land of glory
Staining the land with its neon self-adulation
Rendering truth helpless and despondent

Surrender is not desertion
It is stripping the decoration off a false hero in a pseudo scenario
Refusing to be the pawn in a one-sided chess match
Removing the dusty uniform of "going through the motions"

And walking bare and unquestioning into the land of
empowerment.

Monastery

Within mosaic walls of any dimension
When time was counted with sun and stone
We pledged our life force and eternal submission
Gave every worldly possession owned

In taking vows of servitude, poverty, silence
Became whispers of what we potentially could be
Herding the masses was the intention
Enslave each person by their own decree

Now is the time to take back our freedom
To lessen the yoke of the "powers that be"
Recant the affects of our own self-submission
Realize for ourselves what was cruelly omitted...

"God is alive in the embodiment of me."

Promises

Promises are not copperless pennies collected at the bottom of a purse
Or walked over with indifference
They are little contracts we make for ourselves
A piece of our essence we send out on the road to meet a friend
When we don't show up, we dishonor ourselves
And devalue our own worth
We become ghosts in our own lives
An apparition to our friends who desperately want to believe in us
So they go through the motions...
Taking a receipt for nothing
Nothing
Again and again.

How Did Truth Die?

Truth has gone the way of white bread
The last ingredient on a mass-produced label
Far behind "Agenda" and "Special Interest"
Stretched and distorted with its own special sulphates
Never organic

Truth has become an ancient dialect
There's merely an inflection hinted at in some words
An accent or a spelling...but never the root
Only a distant memory of a people that once spoke it
Did they really exist?

There are stories taught to children
The greatest men of a new land risked all to stake truth's claim
Generations fought and died to preserve it
There are only speculations of
"How did it die?" "When did it die?"

It is no wonder no one understands it
There are only the ridiculous few who believe that it exists
In small inner circles, we seek it out
And know it's not in the bloated intentions of the status quo
Where there have never been any sightings.

Peace on Earth

When the law of the land is to see value in every individual
Not as a collective grunt to dominate...
Control, enslave, imprison, desecrate, invalidate or throw away

But as awesome individuals...each a jewel to cultivate
Compressed from unique experience
Faceted to contribute according to their abilities
Shimmering in their purpose...

Each mind a plethora of knowledge
With the ability to discern and self-govern
Each heart beating in rhythm with humanity
Each being a song with a sacred quality

Always bettering ourselves generation after generation With the
ultimate goal of Life, Liberty and the Pursuit of Happiness for
ALL
Not merely those who have been born with the right skin color,
tax bracket, gender, sexual orientation, etc.

But ALL!
It is then, and only then that we will all be endowed with
Peace on Earth.

Approval

Remove the shunt that feeds approval into your veins
The market price is too high
Buttons, triggers and issues are more visible than you think
Near to the surface and to the left of need.

Release siphoning from others
Dregs of criticism and rebuke are too bitter
To swallow
Not so easy to spit out.

Tap into your own source
You are the mouth of an infinite well
Drink of your own succor
Generously allow others to dip their cup

Only then will your thirst truly be quenched.

Tell someone:
They are beautiful!
Tell someone else:
You are proud of them
Tell someone they are your best friend
Even and especially if they aren't in a human body
Tell someone a time when they helped you in a way that no one
else could
Tell someone you are proud of them
Tell someone you love them

See your power to make a difference through their eyes!

I stand by my conviction to:
Speak kindness where it has never been spoken
Allow others to form their own opinions
Preach *only* to the choir
See greatness where it stands
Respect all souls in all forms
Suspend all judgment...
Bow out of all disagreement
See the world as a wonderful, beautiful place.

Inner Strength

Inner strength is seeing the love and beauty everywhere even though you may not be able to discern it with your physical eyes.

Inner strength is knowing there is possibilities everywhere even when they haven't seemingly come your way.

Inner strength is believing in the goodness in all even though it isn't revealed at first glance.

Inner strength is walking with the absolute intention of making the world a better place with each step.

Inner strength is knowing that you matter and have the ability to uplift humanity merely by showing up with your gifts.

Inner strength is connecting with the heart of love and being that flame of hope, peace and solace for all who know you.

The Moment

The quivering line between horizon and ocean
The magnetic play between stillness and motion
The oil of the sweat of a labor of love
The knee jerk relief when escaping a shove
Ten million moments conjoined in an hour
The disarming grace of a play without power
The biting cry of a fallen bird's call
Recovering your dignity after a fall
The rhythm created when writing a poem
The sanctity felt when journeying home.

Clarity

Gangrene is black
Royal Purple is red
Mass transit is a fancy word for a bus
Child molestation is rape
Status quo is power hoarders pulling strings...
Another form of rape.

You Are

Love personified
A frequency of exhilaration
A single perfect note in the celestial worlds
A beacon
A strain of pure ecstatic bliss
An exclamation of joy!
With a wealth of abundance
Unique point of view
Knowledge with experience sans ego
All the angels in the universe converging in one universal
exclamation of joy!
You are amazing
Grace realized
You are....

The Ultimate Prayer

God doesn't have an ego so doesn't need stroking.

Anything that is written about God is a clumsy, imperfect, attempt to articulate the perfect....It is beyond words.

Man has formulated his concept of God by what he would desire if he were an omniscient being.

There is the conflict.

God has not made man in his own image; man has made God in his.

Think about what you would want for your children.

Would you need them to constantly stroke you, or would you prefer that they were happy and loving and treated their siblings with love and respect?

I think that is a more accurate depiction of what God would "want" if God were capable of wanting.

God wanting, I think, is an outmoded concept.

Be loving and kind to each other.

Respect all of God's gifts.

Listen to God speak within your heart, not in your mind.

Realize your own worth.

Appreciate your own gifts.

Would you like it if everything you gave your children was scoffed at or overlooked?

How about if they destroyed everything they were given?

And every time they were offered an adventure, it was looked at as a punishment?

Connection with God doesn't need to happen in an altered state

Or with super-sensory perceptions.

Everyone is able to connect with God in the natural state of simplicity.

No one is wrong or unworthy to do this.

Take things out of your environment to do this, nothing more needs to be added.

You are perfect in your imperfection,

And gratitude is the ultimate prayer.

Strands

We are greater than our thoughts

Better than the promises we make and break everyday

Far more expansive than our purest joy

Depths and widths beyond our greatest exhilaration...or devastation

We are profoundly more dimensional than an array of skin tones

Incredibly more advanced than conditioning lends us to believe

Exist way below our pay scale

Suffer needlessly at the hands of mass complacency

We diminish ourselves and all life to such a degree

It would be a crime on any other planet

We eat, sleep, and dream in gray and power

That's reflected in our city streets and chambers of our government

To defy convention is to break away from the binding mediocrity

Dream in colors Crayola has never invented

Run barefoot through the fields of original ideas

Unhook the shackles of the fear of looking stupid, standing out

Embrace the depth of our togetherness

As intricate as separate fibers in the same cloth

Together in the freedom of our individual strands

Woven together in the agreement and celebration of a greater cause.

You

You are more dynamic than you believe
Greater than you think
More aware than you reveal
More exhilarating than you feel
And more godly than you realize!

Assistance

I will be your guardian angel
If only you believe
I will heal your deepest anguish
To give you some reprieve

I will unhook you from your troubles
Blow the clouds away
Remove the blight from your eyes
If you only say I may

We will drift to a far off galaxy
Next to the brightest star
I will show you with true vision
The extent of who you really are.

Truth

Truth is not won by drawing a line in the sand
It's etched in the heart what the mind can't withstand

It's forged in a brow all too familiar with pain
Yet too filled with resolve to hold onto disdain

It's not built up in columns or a heavy facade
It follows along the cracks of each meandering "Le Maurade"*

It bleeds through the fibers of the ego's tattered remains
'Til all is bleached unrecognizable but the humility stains

It crumbles the vestige of the smallness of man
Reunites the omega with the alpha, where the individual began.

* A rogue path forged by enthusiasm

Being

The unequivocal distinction between thinking and knowing
The symbiotic relationship between coming and going
The melodic precision of a satisfying resound
Commanding a presence without uttering a sound

A defining conjecture that becomes a decree
Obeying it faithfully, are we really free?
Incredible grace while being under fire
The fortitude it takes to fulfill any desire

The dancing arrangement of atoms of air
Bantering with inconsistencies that aren't really there
Being is being, either close or afar
We all belong somewhere, wherever we are.

Celebrating the Moment of Now

Raise a chalice to your lips
Taste the nectar of love's bliss
Celebrate in the light of the fire within
Dance to the rhythm and brilliancy of love

Whistle a lover's tune in your heart
Where the milk of experience wells
Take a warrior's view and a lover's stance
In the cause of the moment of now

Dreams of worlds basted in gold
Remembered promises kissed with a vow
And secrets unabashedly shared
Are contained in each moment of love

Gain footing on the step you already took
Reach for the branch you're already on
Turn around if you can and look at yourself
Your journey is in the moment of now.

The True Meaning of Christmas

This year I don't want presents
Things I just don't use
Christmas is misinterpreted
And very much abused

A gift is a symbol of our love
Which words cannot reveal
But when greed takes over where love leaves off
The gift loses its appeal

"I love you" are three simple words
That are easy enough to say
But some find it difficult
So say it in another way

I could continue this poem forever
The topic is quite extensive
But I have to go open my presents now
I hope I get something expensive.*

*Jen Ward at age 17.

Peace

Peace is dynamic

It is thriving in contentedness

It's not a static state of no growth

Peace is an undercurrent

A sublime sense of wholeness beneath the activity

It isn't a stagnant balm over the land

Peace is interaction with mutual respect

It is give and take in perfect imperfect symbiosis

Peace is subtle

It isn't an outer decree but an inner recognition

Peace is not as elusive as the Loch Ness monster

It isn't an outer decree

But an inner victory achieved and maintained each moment

Amidst the outer skirmishes

It's a distinction, a discernment

A perpetual acceptance of a higher state

Peace isn't maintained by an absence of turmoil

But a collective decision by all the moving parts

When enough units decide on peace

Summons peace from their depth

Maintain it in their homes and interactions

The balance will be tipped and the collective will spontaneously agree...

That peace is the unspoken law of the land

Peace will then reside in the minds and hearts and will of the people

And *then* settle in the land.

Tears

Drops of truth flow sweetly down the curve of the face
Welling from an infinite source
Where love and pain intermingle in a a swirling pot of memories
Some conscious, some quarantined in a private reserve
Of shame and unworthiness
Their presence is a betrayal to the facade
They seep through the layers of woven protection
That suffocate the breath of joy and dim the inner light
Cutting through to the surface like a fresh wound
Like little ninjas they collect at the edge of the abyss
Balled up in a tuck and roll
Simultaneously tearing off their mask
As they free-fall over the wall to the ultimate surrender
Pay homage to each tear
Each is a testament to an ancient and universal plight
The illusion of separation from the source
The universal cry to belong
And to be collected back into the arms of love.

The Amazing Feat

A man arrived at the pearly gates
Still shaken from his demise
St. Peter greeted him graciously
He was pleasantly surprised

"You are an inspiration here
As we watched your life unfold
Word spread fast about your feat
It was a blessing to behold."

The man did a quick scan of his life
Not quite sure of his amazing task
"Was it my excellence in business?"
He summoned his courage to ask

"Was it my donations to the poor?
Or how I stood my ground?
Was it always giving sound advice?
Or how I worked a crowd?"

"You are all those things, that is correct
All the attributes we here coven
But all here are at least that good
Those traits are a dime a dozen,

"Yet you are honored above the rest

And this I do applaud

You brought a piece of heaven to earth

In how you loved your dog."

Reborn to Love

Just when you feel pushed beyond your limit

Have given beyond your endurance

Been mocked, ridiculed, defiled, and ignored

Unappreciated, underestimated, undervalued, and misunderstood

When you are curled in a ball of exhaustion

Clutching deeply to that last nerve

Or kneeling in a crumpled, heaving mound of tears

Know you are not alone

Know that every great soul who has used every ounce of their beingness to ignite a passion in man...

...Understands

Every great leader, savior, teacher, and innovator knows the journey that you walk

Understands the doorway through which you pass

Has willed themselves over a very similar threshold

Took a respite in the comfort of their faith

Until the last layer of illusion was stripped off them

And they stood stark naked before truth

Their bones picked clean of guilt, want, and pride

Unencumbered, unabashed, unafraid

Determined to give more, determine to thrive, determined to be free

This is the shine

Gleaning from within

Empowered from within

Awakened and alive

Reborn to Love

Realized in Love
Enlightened to Love
Liberated
Loving
Free!

Being Centered Is...

Balance

An alignment with an awareness beyond the limited human consciousness—

While still functioning in daily living

Dipping a straw into wisdom, truth and love

Siphoning it out in a perpetual flow to all

Being the calm eye in the storm of existence

Being the rotational pull on all your thoughts, emotions, actions,

Never wavering from that stance

Never coming out of your center

Waiting for circumstance to be drawn to you

Never running after it

Seeing all situations as concentric circles in which you are their center

You are the sun in your universe

You govern your emotions

You govern your thoughts

You govern your experiences

You own your beingness

You are present every moment

You are free.

You!

You are not who you think you are.

The brain has no idea.

You are not your feelings.

Feelings are very low to the ground.

You are not what you experienced in the past.

You are only a tiny fraction of what you are experiencing in the moment.

You are not limited to the choice of words you chose to use to define yourself.

You are not guilty, ugly, stupid, or fat.

All words are a glass ceiling on the self, especially the negative ones.

We worry about someone diminishing us. They don't need to.

The perpetrator got in. It is an inside job.

We diminish ourselves.

We echo past experiences, relationships, interactions and tragedies and bring them into the sacred moment of now.

We do that.

No one is in our moment doing it to us.

Our presence with ourselves is ours alone. It is our place of love and reverence.

When we say, "They did this to me," then you are doing it to yourself.

When you say, "They told me I can't," you are telling you, you can't.

When you say, "I am clumsy, stupid, useless," you are taking the divine and desecrating it into clumsy, stupid, useless energy.

When you say it about another or yourself, it does not matter. We are all the same. It does not matter if you speak it out loud or say it in your head. It is still in play.

You are the divine.

There are a billion trillion ways to describe it, but it needs to register, or all is lost.

You are every beautiful image.

You are every note of inspiration.

You are every story of adventure.

You are every act of heroism.

You are every pure breath.

You are the moment of truth.

You are a whisper and explosion weaving into each other.

You are the moment of conception.

You are the place where the yin and yang meet and agree.

You are every moment of reaching out to others.

You are every connection.

You are every single note of the divine.

You are an emanation of wonder.

You

You Are:

Nature's talisman,

Every experience of awakening,

A nova expanding into your own galaxy,

Atoms vibrating into sound,

A tapestry of intricacy,

You are realized when you realize

You are God realized.

Buying Freedom

A thousand lives are currency
That convert to a moment of clarity
The pain and frustration we so quickly spend
Is the price of admission for the right to transcend
The disdain that is forged in harboring a lie
Is the apathy built up when we don't even try
The secrets we cling to in our darkest of hour
Constrict us from accessing our personal power
The boundary lines that need to be drawn
Are where the wings of our freedom burst into song
The heights that we attempt to arrive at by foot
Can be reached with one loving intention or look
A dream that jolts us awake and aware
Can wipe out the onslaught of an ominous despair
A murmur becomes an echo that turns into a decree
When the seeker utters the realization that declares, "I Am Free."

Second Sight

Cut away the blind spots
That choke your inner vision
Pain and loss are the site
Of the first incision

Want, craving, hunger, need
Expand the void in which we bleed
Feeding the wish to inspire
Dries the lustful wanton desire

Pay the piper with true coin
Selfless goodness fill the void
As human nature waxes and wanes
Primal impulse starts to refrain

Beyond the calibre of night
Through the vestige of second sight
Partake of the world as it's meant to be
Illuminated, abundant, loving and free.

The Flip Side

If people are lazy...
They are resting.
If people can't seem to care for themselves...
They are healing from a traumatic past.
If people lie...
They are afraid of being called out.
If people steal...
They are feeling depleted inside and think it is their only recourse.
When people are very accomplished...
Many times they are terrified of failing.
When people need to conquer others...
They are trying to fill their own emptiness.
When people are jealous of you...
They admire you greatly.
When people hate you...
They so desperately want your Love.

When we Love, when we Love, when we Love...
We heal all wounds, sooth all traumas, reassure all ills, fill in all voids, and demonstrate the healing power of Love.

The Empath

A word is a container for a feeling or thought
An inaccurate form of conversion
Many manipulate and misinterpret the box
A natural unconscious diversion

Some put a different value on each word
And confuse the going exchange rate
It leaves them stuck in a quagmire of thoughts
Tangled in perpetual debate

Some can take the word-boxes they see
And convert them back into expression
But most are too attached to the box
To know this is a specialized lesson

Some are able to feel the thought
Naked, raw, unabashed
The empath feels everything
Boxless and unattached

An empath can move into the love
Like breath moves through the air
Be a presence wherever love goes
Without a thought even knowing they're there.

Pure Love

I AM a crystal
I AM a tree
I AM a poet
I AM a bee

I AM the ocean
I AM each wave
I AM life's troubadour
Its unbridled knave

I AM the sunshine
That luminates the sea
I AM the moonbeam
I dance upon me

I AM whatever experience
I gratefully allow
I AM the farmer
I AM the plow

I move through each atom
From below and above
I AM capable of all
Because I AM pure love.

You (II)

You exist beyond forever
You're more expansive than the sky
You are valued beyond all measure
You are intelligence beyond the mind
You are joy beyond all pleasure
You are love beyond your heart
You are more than your condition
You're well-scripted beyond your part
You perceive beyond all senses
You're not limited by your lens
When you judge, you get all muddled
Acceptance is the cleanse
When you're still, it opens thresholds
Saying no will close a door
In the raw truth of the moment
You know all this and more.

Integrity

When you give your approval to something you don't agree with,
You are diminishing your own voice.
When you agree to a negative statement,
You are lowering your vibrations.
When you comply just to keep peace,
You give away your power.
When you appease,
You are empowering someone else.
When you say something you don't mean,
You are dissipating your credibility.
When you make a promise that you don't keep,
You are splitting your energy into two streams:
The one you walk and the one you agreed to walk.
When you believe in something without question,
You are giving away your ability to discern.
When you follow out of fear,
You live in fear.
When you preach without the answers,
You preach ignorance.
When people blindly lead,
You have blind followers.
When you find fault,
You are showing yours (faults).
When you show indifference,
You create a wound.
When you ignore,
You create a ghost.

When you dismiss anyone as unimportant,

You just missed an opportunity to truly know your own depth.

What It Is to Be Free

I am a cavern that love pours in
The echo of sound, crisp and full
Beckons me to quench this thirst for truth
With the skill of a craftsman and the eagerness of youth

All my atoms are charged, eager, and lithe
As they expand in rhythm to a greater awareness
Pulling away from the illusion of form
Like the heat of the sun dissipates the girth of a storm

In an altered state, I experience "I Am"
If I can do it, everyone can
My atoms that know that I am inevitably free
Stretch through the universe to know all they can see

While the mind thinks, it's this solid matter
Your atoms are craving permission to scatter
To stretch through the universe as ambassadors of you
Infiltrate your illusion with what's really true

In this way, we all blend and blur
We discover the secret to how to endure
Realizing what we experience, under ego's rule
Is our personal lesson plan in our own private school

In energy we are never so trapped
We go wherever our imagination can see

The only prison that there really can be
It's the mind that can't fathom, what it is to be free.

Section IV: Love

The Love Dial

The Golden Amber of an azure sky
Erases the memory of times gone by

Turn off the news, sit within...
Forget all talk of war and sin

Your heart is a working aperture, a dial if you will
You can get a sense of it while advancing to be still

It's set on "closed" by all the pain you see
But it needs to be open for all to be free

We need to accept the depth of who we all are
Forgo every transgression, being transfixed on each scar

The collective of all needs to undo that dial
Unjar the crust, squeeze out a smile

Forget thinking of factions that pump out the pain
Focus on the goodness of the all that remain

Quiet the fear and memory of loss
Perpetuate truth, love, and kindness, absorb any cost

See...the azure sky is more than fodder for art
It's the beckoning within to a luminous heart

Not just for us or we'd stay wallowing in pride
For all souls who call earth the home they reside

When turning the dial, let the worry rescind
Then love in this world will collectively begin

You can witness the news till you're blue in the face

But it won't heal the world like a pure act of grace

You can beat both your fists until they're bruised, battered, and broken
But it won't be as powerful as when truth is spoken

You can deny all you want through shit eating teeth
But your innocent essence transparently cowers beneath

Just unwind the dial and let it come forth
Accept the stinging reality of knowing your worth

Be one of the unfurling souls coming out from ground cover
Awaken to the connectedness we're anxious to discover

Then all outer circumstances will flip on a dime
Wonder will bloom, inner music will chime

Then everyone everywhere may start to agree
In this powerful intention for the collective "we"

Maybe you'll feel love not just for those that you bore
But for every single stranger on the way to the store

And as pure love pumps out from that perpetual old well
The concept of truth, love, and kindness will be easy to sell.

Question on Love

Do you feel it
The warm glow of the body
Like being tucked into bed in new pajamas after a bath
Do you hear it
The excitement of the peepers on the first warm night
Crickets itching their leg in unison
Do you smell it
In the smoky fire that means security in the primal tongue
Do you see it
In the kind gestures that you are witness to
Do you feel it
In the soft skin and fur of your loved ones
Do you sense it
In the hum of the atoms and the harmony of nature
Do you appreciate it
In each breath that anchors your light to matter
Do you share it
In the many unique qualities you have accrued through
experience
Do you believe it as your truth
Do you embrace it as a virtue
Do you own it as your center
Do you define it in your presence
Do you recognize it every moment
Do you perceive its depth
Conceive it as a concept
Hold a place for it in this world

Cherish it beyond all reason
Perpetually channel it forth
Mimic and personify it
To know yourself and all through it
YES!

Love's Appeal

Tell me I don't matter
Tell me you don't care
Tell me it's all bullshit
That you're not really there

Tell me there's no freedom
That everything's a lie
Carelessly chuckle and walk away
As you watch me die inside
Or...
Tell me there is purpose
In all we say and do
Give me reason to believe
In love, in life, in you

Plant a garden with your words
Make each day a song
Give all a reason to exist
Tell us we belong

Give all purpose, don all truths
Make all scenarios win/win
From the ashes of defeat
Sprouts of Providence begin

See peace when others envision war
Talk advantage when others spout loss

Risk vulnerability and feeling raw
Show kindness at any cost

Encourage, enlighten, visualize, evolve
Empathize, appreciate, heal
Cater to one's sense of higher truth
To deliver love's appeal

It doesn't really matter
What you say or do
As long as you act from the depth of love
And know that place is you.

Love Play

Power strutted its stuff in front of love
Love noticed its beautiful eyes
Power punched love in the shoulder
Love stroked power's face
Power haughtily mocked Love
Love smiled sweetly in return
Power tried to wrestle love to the ground
Love made the sign of peace and backed away
Power bullied, complained, and tried to manipulate love
Love merely watched power
Power tried to pull love into a pit of despair
Love stepped back
Power cried victim and spit venom at Love

Love hugged power and walked away

Power used up all its life force in selfish pursuits

Love healed all the victims of power with kindness

And danced into the hearts of all.

Love's Scribe

Love Doesn't Care...

What religion you are

What you have done in the past

The color of your skin

Your political affiliations

Who you love

What you look like

How many cookies you eat

How you have compensated for feeling unloved

Where you live

What clothes you wear

How tall you are

How athletic you are

If you watch too much TV

To...

Guilt you at all

Shame you

Diminish you

Demoralize you

Isolate you

Judge you

Blame you

Whither away your sense of self

Punish you

Pit you against others

Deface you

Separate you from others

Dry up all hope

Crush your dreams

Weaken your conviction

Lesson your hope

These are things that man is responsible for...the lesser side of man

Love does not endorse man to do these things. Ego and power are the driving force in every way, shape and form. Love tries to deter these things even by using us as scribes for Love's true purpose

Love...

Supports you

Cheers on your victories

Comforts you through defeats

Introduces you to the greater part of your self

Allows you to see love in all

Encourages you

Makes you know in your heart of hearts that you are special

Encourages you to...

Speak your truth

Live with purpose

Love at all costs

Follow your dreams

Give without reserve

Taps you into an infinite place of bounty

Allows you to see yourself in all others

Allows you to connect to all others

Allows you to teach, heal, inspire and thrive

Helps you recognize your purpose

Gives you the courage to live your purpose

Gives you the wisdom to see yourself as love, too

Allows you to be permeated with love

Sends you out in the world as its ambassador

Meets you in a million guises

Becomes you.

9/15/15

Love's Beautiful Array

Hazel blue
Amber gray
It's only pigment
Anyway

Cinnamon brown
Or almond skin
They're not tinctures
On the love within

Either ruby lips
Or pale brown
Love's sweet kiss
In both resounds

Flaccid loose
Or pulled real taunt
It's merely love's camouflage
That is flaunt

New Agers
Or conservative in thought
Merely live the love
As they are taught

Why can't we all stop
To realize
Love has no color
Age or size

It has no preference
There is no sin
We all look the same
From within

We all think the same
From our heart
There's no need for vantage points
To drive us apart

When someone is different
It is an opportunity to see
Love's beautiful array
From the Universal "WE"
8/17/15

Love in the End

Solar flares

Winter blues

Indian summer

Deja vu

Quiet outbursts

Putting allegations to bed

Are we guided by Angels

Or just randomly led

Each season's solstice

Swimming up creek

Finding answers to questions

Dismissed by the meek

Desiring to go further

Than your leash will allow

Finding God in all places

Even in worshiping a cow

Searching all temples

Revisiting all shrines

Is your God the real one

Or is it mine

Standing on a pulpit
Or shouting from the street
Find Love in all places
Shake hands when you meet

Nature or nurture
It doesn't really matter
If you feel God's love is innate
Or is won by your flatter

When your blood, brains and bones
Are put into the ground
It's the "you" that is left
That still hovers around

Ascends into heaven
Re-acclimates
Remembers it's been there
Revisits its fate

It does it all over
Again and again
Until you realize each moment
That we're all love in the end.

Love Is All You Are

A thousand feet away
Is all the joy you need
Take that one short journey
You deserve it in Godspeed

A hundred feet away
Is all the love you can endure
It is your own base nature
Because your heart is pure

Twenty feet away
I know it's hard to believe
Is the abundance of all riches
Just be ready to receive

A few short steps away
Freedom is in your grasp
Have you the nerve to take it
Do you even have to ask

Step into your center
Why did it take so long
Joy, Love, Abundance are your birthright
Freedom is your song

Take off the garbs of illusion
Matter, energy, time and space
You are oh so everything
Being you is a loving place

Reunite with all the wonder
Collect love on you like the dew
It's magnetically attracted to
Everything you think, feel, say and do

Feel love in your atoms
Pulsing through your very veins
Love is all you are, see, hear and feel
And everything that remains

See how important the journey is
In the lifespan of every soul
It helps us realize we are immersed in love
That being love in the only goal

We are actually always love
Being the opposite is the illusion
Thinking we are separated
Is what creates all the confusion

But when you listen to your heart

Ignoring the limited mind resolve

Love will be your everything

So let everything else dissolve.

6/30/15

Love's Call - Dedicated to You

What must I say to inspire you
What do you need to feel loved
How can I convince you of the magnitude of your worth
What else in words can be said

I see all the pain that you carry
All the times you had to go it alone
All the memories you hold of being beaten or scorned
I watched as your heart turned to stone

I cheer you for your attempts to melt it
By focusing on a special someone
How can I make you understand that you've never been lost
Love bathes you effortlessly as the sun

Your tears were never a cry in the dark
They are a great means of flushing out pain
You are learning each moment the depth of your worth
To meet challenges without a hint of disdain

You now know you are more than an island
Or a stranger living unnoticed where you dwell
You are an infinite ember in a perpetual blaze
Not only Godlike but a God atom or cell

You carry all the attributes of Divinity
You display them well when you are "in love"
The trick is to realize that love comes from within
Not from without or above

Glean that special feeling of being in love
Except learn that it comes from the self
Don't just wear it when you have a partner
Then put it once again on the shelf

Let love emanate from your very atoms
Let it shine on your skin like fresh dew
Let it whisper in and kiss your sweet ear
Let it help you realize that it's you

You hold all the keys to what you pray for
Guard the gate to your own inner realm
You are the Master of your divinity
You are the captain at the helm

Steer yourself always to more of your true essence
In your workplace, society, and home
Never do you need to search to find love
Never again must you roam

See Love reflected in nature

From each blade of grass to each tree

Never does it waver from its purpose

Never does it cry out, "Poor Me!"

You are a graceful display of personified awesomeness

An inspiration to one and to all

You are respected and admired beyond all reproach

Simply by hearing and heeding Love's call.

9/8/15

NO...Just Say No

No life is disposable.

No one is unworthy of help.

There is no such thing as a lost cause.

Though struggle is valuable for growth, watching others walk away leaves its mark.

No one is not worth helping.

No time spent helping is a waste.

No one is too important to not give a damn.

Spirituality is no excuse for apathetic indifference.

There is no one that is so scarred and broken that they don't respond to love.

There is no kindness that is too small.

There is no kind word that is not worth mentioning.

There is nothing that can't be healed.

There is no one that cannot be revived.

There is no greater purpose than giving yourself to helping others.

There is no greater crime than giving up on anyone.

There is no greater responsibility than staying open to love.

There is no way to fail except in giving up.

Stand Still

When was the moment in time when you suddenly became so
scared

Do you remember the exact day you realized you didn't care

When was the moment you decided to exist instead of live

Did it coincide in any way with when YOU refused to give

Why did you shut your heart to the beauty of the day

Instead of being a thorough fair, you made your heart one way

When did you forget to feel the enthusiasm to awaken

Was it when you thought someone loved you back and found
out you were mistaken

Life and love are messy...we fall and we collide

We hang on to resentments when we think we've been denied

But others are doing the best they can, hanging on by their shear
will

They never really meant to hurt you...they are not trying to hurt
you still

They are bruised and they are battered from desperately seeking
love

Their natural state to slip into, as a silk lined velvet glove

They hold on to a memory, resent what they can't feel

Believing somehow it's owed to them, they go about to steal

But love is not the type of thing that can be taken much for granted

It's not something you need to search for...there's plenty where you're planted

Stop looking for love as it looks to others and find what is meant for you

It permeates your heart and mind and everything you do

Love is the natural byproduct of doing what you like best

It's not something that you need to prove or win by passing a test

It's not a narrow expression met by just one set of eyes

It's everything that happens, the mundane, as well as the surprise

So here is the secret to recognizing love for the over-zealous mind

Simply drop out of all of the desperate search...then set your sites on being kind

Love will walk right up to you and easily overtake you

It'll easily sweep you off your feet like it was always meant to

Love isn't found by hunting it down or conquered by sheer will

You will find you are immersed in Love...when you just stand still.

6/16/15

The Fight

I am a devoted Champion of Love
If only in my own mind
I dig the trenches and fight the good fight
In ruthless defense to be kind

I undo the damage that's been done
From each powerful selfish decree
I heal the wounds of all that are suffering
Or perhaps just the suffering in me

I can't condone the apathy in man
A display of ignorance's defense
I can only abide so long by the rules of illusion
And condone the systemic pretense

I will continue to do what I do
How else could I possibly endure?
Someone must heal the ills of all men
Until each individual finds their own cure.

11/17/15

The Apathy of Man

Who I Am is not forged
In flesh or words or pride
Who I AM is drawn much deeper
From the ethereal world I reside

Who I AM is not crushed
By mock or scorn or slight
Whatever devastates the external me
Melts away through my celestial flight

Who I AM reminds all others
They themselves beyond mortal stone
Who they are runs much deeper
Than the trespasses for which they atone

You and I are not the script
To which we have beholden so well
You and I are absolute truth
Reflections of the heavens we dwell

You and I are Angelic Captains
Navigating a sea of Sound and Light
Whatever realities we conjure up
Melt away through our second sight

You and I are co-creators
Of this crazy illusion we're living in
We have all co-written the story line
Of hate and greed and sin

Yet, no matter how long we've vested in the journey
It's not too hard to see
When we wince real hard and wipe the crust from our eyes
What we envision this world to be

You and I as creative beings
Have been given a new task
To crumple old blueprints of this world
Strip power of its walls and masks

Create a new vision of a new earth
Where all are empowered and free
The Love and the Light of our true home
Will be written in this new earth's decree

This one small task is entrusted to us
The Awakening of a new realm
You and I are co-creators
Responsible for steering the helm

You and I must show the whole world

Through kindness, beauty and truth

The world that they once envisioned

In the reckless days of their youth

You and I have emerged from the mist

There is no use trying to go back

We have agreed to show all other souls

The love and the joy that they've lacked

This is exciting times to partake in

This alchemy in which we take part

To transform the throbbing apathy of man

Into a golden heart.

10/5/15

The Defense

I met life in a beaded gown
With edges that were frayed
It was my only armor
From power and its play

The garb was awkwardly comfortable
As I wore it just like skin
It was so familiar I didn't know
Where it ends and I begin

As I was met with cruelty
I added beads and knots
It sheltered me from the pain
Hid the real me that I forgot

Then someone smiled sweetly
And wiped my brow of need
In that act of kindness
My dress dropped a single bead

This loosened up the fibers
Seams started splitting all apart
Then a miracle happened
The worn threads exposed my heart

I then received more kindness
The whole dress became unbound
Lost were all defenses
All the beads dropped to the ground

When I watched them tumble
And was stripped of my attire
I realized hate, fear and dread
Are never more required

I stand here bare to the soul
With no other false enhancement
May others too drop their garbs
For the sake of Humanity's advancement

Now I wear a beadless gown
With no hint of wear or fray
Soul is woven in pure Light and Sound
Love shines through to all this way.
8/13/15

The Flip Side

If people are lazy...

They are resting

If people can't seem to care for themselves...

They are healing from a traumatic past

If people lie...

They are afraid of being called out

If people steal...

They are feeling depleted inside and think it is their only recourse

When people are very accomplished...

Many times they are terrified of failing

When people need to conquer others...

They are trying to fill their own emptiness

When people are jealous of you...

They admire you greatly

When people hate you...

They so desperately want your Love

When we Love, when we Love, when we Love...

We heal all wounds, sooth all traumas, reassure all ills, fill in all voids and demonstrate the healing power of Love.

4/27/14

The Miracle of You

Kindness is my prayer
Encouragement is my song
Sincerity is my anthem
Singing it makes me strong

Connectedness is my motto
Service is my decree
Helping others is my virtue
Doing so sets me free

Taking is sometimes giving
Receiving graciously is a gift
Justice is spontaneous
The law of Love works swift

Everything you think
Everything you do
Is meant to excel you further
Into the miracle of you

If denial is your option
Ignorance is it, too
Intelligence isn't awareness
That's what smart people misconstrue

Awareness leads from the heart
Intelligence may follow
A good mind without the heart
Can leave one cold and hollow

But a heart with pure intention
Has warmth and depth to spare
That is how they're recognized
They have ample love to share.
5/17/15

The Moment

The intersection of time and space

Where yin and yang totally agree

Everything and nothing collide

The blind spot ignorance can't see

Where alpha and omega merge

Any understanding will actually be

Where someone meets their true self

To realize they are already free

There is gauged a perspective

Like on the pinnacle of a hill

Everything comes into focus

Perpetual motion becomes still

Where Universal law

Bends to the bias of no decree

The wonders of joy, love and abundance

Are as affluent as can be

You become the windfall

In the beautiful expansion beyond the mind

Existence is the true bounty

In reconnecting with love's kind. 5/3/15

I Stand by My Conviction to:

Speak kindness where it has never been spoken

Allow others to form their own opinions

Preach ONLY to the choir

See greatness where it stands

Respect all souls in all forms

Suspend all judgment

Bow out of all disagreement

See the world as a wonderful, beautiful place.

Divine Love

The resolve after time has eroded the pain

Silt of wisdom to escape an eddy

The body and blood of the anointed... coursing through the veins of humanity

Being strewn between the ebb and flow of birth and death

Continuously smashed against the rocks

Yet maintaining the resiliency to smile

The last note of the ultimate epiphany

That resonates above the highest octave

And whistles as a single note through the heart of a believer.

Love Itself

God was Bored

So he created a game for himself.

He separated all his atoms and allotted them all a different vantage point.

He created a game board out of matter and energy.

Most of his atoms were in on the game. They would stay in the form of love but be disguised as backdrop.

The playing pieces would be the humans; they would think they were most important but also feel separate and lonely.

There would be two identical kinds of players, but they would see each other as inferior.

They would see everything as inferior. This was part of the game.

He gave them the ability to reason so that they could play the game.

They were given feelings so God could experience the game through their vantage point.

They needed a way to move around the board. God created space and time.

Each turn was a lifetime.

Each lifetime they would conquer the other players.

They believed the different playing pieces were given clues to the game that they didn't have.

This was true. Both playing pieces had different strengths that were clues.

They would pair up sometimes as a means of figuring it out.

They would go on tangents for many turns thinking the game was about the pairing up with a particular player.

The pieces started out as ruthless.

They would destroy everything to figure out the rules.

But as they went along each turn, they started to care about the pieces they paired up with.

They would pause from the game and experience real moments of Joy and Love.

Each time they had these moments, they broke through the illusion.

At first, when the reality of Love shone through, they used this to show superiority over the other players.

They gave the other players false clues and a whole set of rules needed to break through the illusion, too.

They called this religion.

Religion would send the other players on wild goose chases for many turns.

But some players still got through the maze.

They started to realize they were in a game.

They started to help the other players instead of working against them.

This washed away more illusion.

God became enthralled in the more advanced players.

This helped them figure out the illusion of space and time...

that the board itself was not real.

More and more players are becoming self-realized.

Figuring out the key to advancing was in not making it about advancing.

Opting out of the rules of power by instilling kindness as their first impulse.

Loving others and forgoing self-contempt by turning the love on themselves.

Surrendering all the rules of the hierarchy of the game.

Being loving and kind in every way that they can while seeped in the game.

Recognizing themselves as love itself.

How to Win the Human Race

I love you through all eyes
Feel you through all skin
Hold you through all arms
Am happy when you win

I cry when you are sad
Hurt when you feel pain
Shine on you like the moon
I wax and then I wane

You have no real enemies
No reason for disgrace
You are loved beyond your station
You are loved beyond your race

There's no need to be diminished
No reason to feel small
Living scared or helpless
Serves nobody at all

We all began believing
We were separate and alone
And that we had these sins to bear
For which we must atone

But Love rushed through and washed away
The smallness that we hide
It broke through all defenses
To free the love inside

It ignited every ember
Like the one inside of you
To exonerate all trespasses
And let that love pierce through

See, it never was about
Walking aimlessly alone
It was experiencing every vantage point
Of which you thought you must atone

It is learning true compassion
For every form of life
Sometimes as the husband
Sometimes as the wife

Once you can truly know
What's going on with another
Then every different form of life
Truly is your brother

And when that happens to us all...

There's compassion for the rest

The heart of humanity will burst forth

We'll have passed the final test

We all together will transcend

Walking hand in hand

Integrity and kindness

Will ring throughout the land

Everything we've done so far

We will totally erase

We will finally stop the madness

And win the human race.

5/14/15

H20

We curse the water for pouring down
We blame it all for freezing
We curse it when it floods the ground
We curse it every season

We blame it when it collects in clouds
When its downpours steal our thunder
We poison it with toxic waste
And rob it of its wonder

We pour crude sugar in each glass
To make it much more tasteful
We desecrate its purity
Abuse it and are wasteful

Taking for granted what is vital to us
May be part of our decline
Others can dis what's 75% of them
I will be grateful for mine.
7/11/14

Encouragement of a Full Moon

Stand between the Sun and Moon
Let the Love and Light pass through
Illuminate your bountiful heart
Drop the extraneous part called you

Magnify your bountiful heart
To the size and width of earth
Treat it as a looking glass
To show others their ultimate worth

Hold up the mirror to their giant group heart
Brace as they cringe and recoil
Pour love into the very essence of all
Drain all the dross out into the soil

Hold the reflection steadily
Ignore the negative onslaught
Love breezes clean every last atom
Before its true essence is caught

Be unwavering as the Moon and the Sun
Match their luminescent light
Allow others to realize the brilliancy of truth
By accessing their own second sight

Span across the globe of man
Rise above the stagnant air
Pierce the earth with your magnified love
Let it feel the extent of your care.

Become one with the body of earth
Let the Sun and Moon's light pass straight through
Expand the atoms to an omniscient state
Allow truth to align in you

Be the surrogate of the highest purpose
In the humanity of man
Yes it's possible to help the world transcend
Just by being aware that you can.

8/11/14

A Distant God

I'd like to meet most any God that isn't based on Love
And show him what he's doing to earth, as push has come to shove

He must have turned his head away when his message was set in cause
There's such an inconsistency between Love and the obeying of his laws

Maybe he had a vision that just got misconstrued
To have a noble intention in everything we do

There might be a miscommunication that has to be set straight
Any God worth his weight preaches Love, not hate

Maybe it's the interpretation as so many are steeped in sin
It's not about conquering the world, but going quietly within

It's not about seeing the faults of others, "Bringing them to their knees"
It's seeing Love in everyone...let them worship as they please

God had this pure intention...all must realize
It was man who's buried it in ritual and covered it with lies

Any God that is a God, that is instilled in the hearts of man
Doesn't incite the world in violence...Love has another plan

Teach responsibility in everything you do
If you judge for your God, that transgression is on you

I can't agree with any man who diminishes others for God
But I realize the learning curve...it's the reverence I applaud

There is also a huge lesson, bookmarked just for me
I can't micromanage everyone...I must just let them be

If I have judgment in what another is ensuing
Then I am doing exactly what I accuse them of doing

If I question what someone values in a cynical maraud
I myself am worshiping a distant unloving God.

Every Angel

I gazed upon a feather
Just to know its charms
The down barbules waved rhythmically
Like tiny little arms

They showed a flexibility
Its quill a quiet stance
From this new perspective
Began a new romance

Because once you truly see something
Take it in from all directions
It's nearly quite impossible
To not develop true affections

This is a key to mastering Life
A skill one can depend
The means to unfurl such beautiful wings
And finally to transcend

If you can look at anyone
Beyond all pain and strife
Become enamored with their quiet virtue
Then you can love all life

No longer will you be imprisoned
Grounded by the Id
You will become immortal
Like every Angel did.
5/21/15

The Golden Thing...

The golden thing society sees
Is just the love flowing through me
It's not in the norm yet flows through each form
It's the "what" and the "will" I AM to be

It starts as a hum and grows to crescendo
And soon the day will be...
When the world remembers the Light and the Love
And forgets the synthetic me.

The Tiny Fleet of Sandy Hook Angels

A tiny fleet of Angels
Graced the world one day
Seven years they walked the earth
Immersed in children's play

We thought we knew their purpose
To be nurtured and uplift
Each assigned a special family
With which to share their gifts

Each child is like a song of God
A sacred celestial tone
But the music ended abruptly one day
God called his Angels home

Now the world feels cheated
Because of what transpired
How could death so cruelly take
What heaven has inspired?

But the world has gone complacent
Indifferent to the core
With this devastating wake-up call
The golden rule can be restored

God in his infinite wisdom
Set sights on something grand __

To restore the milk of human kindness
In the brotherhood of man

These children are etched in our hearts
On a canvas made of pain
Yet, where the gully of anguish is carved
Their innocence remains

This tiny fleet of angels
That reawakened the heart of man
Is the golden instrument to mark and gauge
Where Peace on Earth began.

Dance to the Rhythm of Love

Raise a chalice to your lips
Taste the nectar of love's bliss
Celebrate in the light of the fire within
Dance to the rhythm of love

Dreams of worlds basted in gold
Remember promises kissed with a vow
And secrets unabashedly shared
Are contained in each moment of love

Gain footing on the step you already took
Reach for the branch you're already on
Turn around if you can and look at yourself
Your journey is in the moment of now.

Love

Love scampers around our homes with furry feet
and minor demands
Revealing its ultimate purpose

Stay in the moment----feed me
Stay in the moment----walk me
Stay in the moment----pet me

Each disgruntled compliance
Whittles away our indifference
Until the ultimate realization

It doesn't matter if love is in us or around us
If we can feel it without, we can experience it within
Love is no longer feral

Good boy
Good boy.

Genius

Let your genius burn a hole in convention
Radiate it out in a searing, singeing, smoldering awareness
Rest once in a while to tap off the ash of indifference

The "what ifs?"
The "shoulds"
And the "could have beens"

Pay no mind to the dancing little embers that waft off into the
sky
The ones that make others wince
They secretly squint in awe and publicly scoff in contempt

Pleading in silent prayer that one will land upon the edge of their
pain
Ignite it to passion
So that they can recognize and claim their own brilliance
Life's equation

You are the sum of all your experiences
Heartache, lust and glory bracketed by lifetimes
Multiplied by resilience
Compiled in a form as limiting as a number

You are the ultimate resolve
Pooled and planted in the illusion of one form

The vastness and fortitude of God limited only by your ability
To realize your own depth

You fraction your own greatness in relation to your acceptance
level
Your greatness is the whole number
Acceptance is the common denominator
You are love squared.

Kindness

I came here with a pure heart
The world tainted it
I spit venom
It stained my soul
I convulsed in pain

Kindness picked me up and unclenched my fists
It dusted off the accrued layers
It washed my tear-stained face
It taught me how to mimic its smile
It reminded me of my own light

I became kind
I started to pick up others
To wash their stained faces
Undo the venom that I once spewed

To heal their hearts

I will leave here with a pure heart.

Love's Compassion

Hate saw Love and was enraged
Love saw Hate and felt compassion
Hate shook its fist at Love
Love kept its distance out of deference
Hate attacked Love but lost its balance and fell
Love kept its composure
Hate cried
Love answered its call
Love helped Hate up
Hate looked at Love and was confused
Hate thought that it was Love
Hate now knew what Love looked like
Hate melted into Love at the realization
Love collected itself and went on its way.

The Whole Story

Wisdom helped Pride up after the fall
Peter was glad Paul got paid
The right hand always knew what the left was doing
Push and Shove talked and then shook hands
Time was actually a gift from her parents
The dog was too engaged to learn another trick
The fat lady lost 200 pounds and opened her own show
The ducks all fell in a row when they were left alone
The torch wasn't being held for someone, it was being passed
Love is a good thing and it never ends.

Beauty

There's no need to travel to where beauty dwells
It springs abundantly from an infinite well
Not a place that one needs to see
More of a presence, and learning to just "be"
Opening the doorway of a stillness, walking inside
Finding the Law of Love easy to abide
Seeing your inner presence so crystal, so clear
Your own sacred intention diffusing all fear
Walking the edge between consciousness and fate
Defying conformity at an alarming rate
Finally seeing what was already there
The love and beauty you see is your own private mirror.

Be Perpetual Love!

Blow your wad of greatness into the world
Spend it like a drunken sailor
Burn it up
Like the last inch on a molten candle

Let your flame dance in the night
Unhindered by fear of the damp air of darkness
Hoard away nothing of yourself
To leave decayed in the attic of regret

Lose yourself in the process of giving
Live in the perpetual flow
Feel yourself expand in the exponential propulsion of your being
Immersing in the exhilaration of unadulterated love.

Gift of Love

What if God sent you a gift of pure love to add for your life?
Would you refuse it?
Would you over-scrutinize it?
Would you send it away?

Why would you send it away?
Because it didn't come in a form you expected?
Did you not recognize it?
Was it inconvenient?
Did you feel unworthy?

Every time Love wanders into your life in the form of a new relationship, it is a gift from God
Pets are love personified
To refuse a pet is to turn down a gift of love.

Awakening

Within crusted walls of embedded emotion
Bombarded by waves of perpetual commotion
Is a permanent "me" determined to stand
Slough off adversity like layers of sand

Draw in the light from a far away source
To stand firm in the love seems par for the course
Reverberating in music, a most precious choir
Break through the dross, confusion, and mire

Emanate, vibrate, reverberate, resound
Inundated with such beauty, I unfurl and rebound
Showing others imprisoned what awakening can be
Humbly resonating beautiful and free.

Spiritual Marriage

Positive, Negative
Soul equals Soul
Masculine, Feminine
Eternity's the goal

The same, yet different
Together, apart
Companionship matters
Compatibility as art

Expecting nothing
Desiring the same
Learning, changing
Both in pure Love's name

Separate units
Nothing guaranteed
Love most divine
Everything is free.

You Are Love

You are love
You don't need to chase it
Or defend it
You don't need to have it validated
You don't have to feign illness to be loved
You don't have to be in pain
You don't have to be rich, pretty, or successful to be love
You don't have to perform to be worthy
Being needy does not draw it to you
You don't have to feel it, to be it
You don't have to be demonstrative in love
You don't have to have it reflected in the eyes of a lover
All of life is reflecting love back to you
All you have to do is take off your blinders
Forgo your resistance to it
Release quantifying love in yourself and others
Stop running away from it by trying to run towards it
Surrender the fight
Give up the search and rescue
Flick that chip off the shoulder
Drop that bundle of rationale
Remove all the masks you've been wearing
Lay down the sword and shield
Crumble the wall you have been building
Drop your arms
Unclench your fists
Relax your atoms

Merely surrender to love

You will recognize love the moment you stop looking in the horizon

And gaze upon your own essence

Not with the physical eyes

But the eyes and heart of Soul.

The Nature of Love

Love doesn't hate Hate

If Love hated Hate it would not be Love

If Love hated Hate, Love would fold itself into Hate

But then it would not be Love

Love is not afraid of Hate

Love has compassion for Hate

Love realizes that Hate is merely an absence of itself

If Love withheld itself from Hate, it would be perpetuating Hate

To dissipate Hate,

Love realizes it must give Love to Hate

So Love loves Hate and melts Hate back into Love

Love acknowledges all and sees only Love reflected back to it.

Special Child

A few short years ago she came to be
In the path of our family way
God sent her on special angel wings
And we thank Him every day

For her golden beauty
Is more than in her face
It's in her look and thoughtfulness
And hopefully in our grace

She fills the darkest mood with light
And waivers wrong to right
In the other children's eyes
Brings a look of sheer delight

For other children see her for what she is
A gift from heaven above
The rest of us see what we'd like to be
A pure expression of love.

Jen Ward at age 17

Dear Mom,

I'm tired of all the cards
That tell of a mother's care
How especially thoughtful they are
And how their love's so rare.

They tell of deep devotion
A divinity that's true...
But Mom they don't know the half of it
Because they don't know you.

It's not the things you gave me
Though those were real nice, too
It's more the things you taught me
To help my love shine through.

 Like treating all people equal
Not thinking I am best
To not treat some as special
While ignoring all the rest.

You taught me what is real
and what is just pretense
and loving those who don't love me
Is my best defense.

So Mom,

Thank you for the freedom
For the love and care
Thank you for the wisdom
That in mortals is sometimes rare.

And as we walk the path of life
And our missions keep us apart
Know you are alive in my memories
And dancing in my heart.

Engaging Love

Love in the abstract
Yet keep it in your mind
Wrap it around your shoulders
Wear it as divine

Feel it in your fingers
Share it on your tongue
Leave its mark on strangers
Feed it to your young.

Melting into Love

I don't want to hurry awake because I want to remember my dreams

I don't want to jump into my routine. I want to bask in the joy of the new light of day.

I don't want to hurry through feeding my furry family. I want to savor them savoring their meal.

I don't want to be distracted when I am listening to someone. I am honored that they trust me with what is important to them.

I don't want to skimp when feeding the squirrels and birds. I want to gift them with the experience of abundance.

I don't want to hold back when sharing truth. I respect everyone too much to dilute myself to appease them.

I don't want to diminish my experiences or other people by throwing labels on them. That is one step away from dismissing them.

I don't want to run through life blindly because I don't want to miss one opportunity to give solace, an insight, or a kindness when it's truly needed.

I don't want to cross over thinking that I could have loved, healed or shared more than I have.

I don't want to leave anything of myself on the table. I want to melt into love for all times.

12/6/15

Being Invisible

Is there more love and light to give
When beauty fades with its last chagrin?
When power plays have come and went
And natural resources have all been spent?

When friends and calls are far between
And contributions go unseen?
When all that's left is that one last hope
That there's more beyond the human scope?

The human canvas is camouflage
Not a storage tank for ensilage
Providence happens in a higher place
As love smooths the brow of a weary face.

Combustion

Love is like a volatile gas

It is ready to ignite at the lightest movement
The slightest touch
The smallest whisper

People are afraid of its power so they insulate it well within
They surround it on all sides by walls and deflections
They are terrified that others may see its volatile influence upon
them
They dilute it with pain and self contempt

But love was meant to be combustible
It is meant to ignite in everyone and everything
It is meant to spread its noxious gas of spontaneous joy and
appreciation
And contaminate all with perpetual optimism and approval

The world is meant to be infected by love
It has experienced every form of disease and perversion
Now it is time to lay down in the poppy field, gather up one's
dispersions
And feast on the underlying condition of self-acceptance

The fear and contempt is too great for the masses to uphold
They are ready to relinquish the ultimate control in the quest for
power
And resign themselves to the simplicity and serenity of the
ultimate truth
Love is innate and more permeating than power

Love is the ultimate conduit, sanctum, and expression of self

Love is the arrival and achievement of the ultimate quest

Love is the wholeness of completeness

Love is all and nothing combined

Love is...nothing else matters.

Integrity's By-Laws

Heaven is won by the blessings we share
Hell is decreed when we show we don't care
Improve to establish a better set of laws
By acknowledging others' greatness instead of their flaws

How we treat others
Is our personal cadence
A unique brand of kindness
Our own providence

In a world that is seeped in the depth of illusion
Where those who see truth are called out for delusion
They fall into indignities of society's bad grace
Their wisdom, the egg on conformity's face

We call forth the honor
Of Integrity's creed
The innate love we ache for
For which we all bleed

Cast away the demons
That leave us all blind
Return to the love
Leave all transgressions behind

Open your heart
Pull out love's reserve
Rewrite the by-laws
Of what we deserve.

Your Donation

Open up the floodgates
Between the human and divine
Rest yourself in sweat-stained sheets
Let your ego lay supine

Offer yourself up to the heavens
That beckon you to undress
The real self walks in brilliant wonders
That the mind cannot suppress

Bring a gift back to this world
A memory or insight
Leave it as a "bread crumb trail"
So others may take flight.

I Pledge...

I pledge devotion to the world
And all the souls who inhabit it
And to the Source
Which we all are connected
One world
Imbued with God
Individualized
With abundance and freedom
For all.

When You:

Say yes, you open a door
Agree, you perpetuate harmony
Smile, you pour love into this world
Return a smile, you are in agreement with love
Support, you strengthen a cause
Encourage, you nurture a conviction
Love everyone, everyone loves you
See beauty, you are beautiful
Look past faults, you see truth
Acknowledge a voice, hear a song
Ask how, the universe will show you
Are grateful, you unfurl your wings.

Empowerment

A quiet whisper in the night
A vision formed from second sight
An awareness beyond all sense of reason
As certain as the turn of the coming new season

The calm that's a surrender beyond compare
The need to reach out when no one is there
The will to live, not merely survive
Tasting one's tears to prove one's alive

The hope that awakens a perpetual bliss
The ecstasy triggered in the first kiss
Seeing your future in someone's eyes
Finding new love, life's pleasant surprise.

Diatribe

Demand to be heard
Stomp around on this earth
Kick up the dusty facade
Break through the floorboards
Free fall through the rafters
Tap dance in the air
Read to the sprites
Bow to the applause
Make strides in all directions
Catch a glimpse of your greatness in the side mirror
You are closer than you appear
Take lucid breaths
Write your own anthem and toss it in the wind
Put an exclamation point on every sentence!
Mark your existence with a yellow highlight
Be a symphony
Be a riddle
Be a one-person act that none can follow
Be the love
Be that haven in someone's storm
Donate a penny for their thoughts
See their pain in your eyes
Reflect back kindness
Milk the sweetness
Make no apologies
Make a mess of things
Forgive yourself

Rest
Rest in the arms of love.

Loved on all Sides

You don't need an agenda
You don't need a cause
You don't need a platform
To draw in applause

You don't need to be seen
You don't need to be heard
You don't need to do anything
That belief is absurd

You don't need to prove anything
To show what you're worth
You've been loved beyond measure
Eons before your last birth

You are cradled in acceptance
Nestled in love
It may not feel so from below
But you're complete from above

You are cheered on by angels
Mentored by guides

Accepted unconditionally
Loved on all sides.

Question on Love

Do you feel it?
The warm glow of the body
Like being tucked into bed in new pajamas after a bath
Do you hear it?
The excitement of the peepers on the first warm night
Crickets itching their legs in unison
Do you smell it?
In the smoky fire that means security in the primal tongue
Do you see it?
In the kind gestures that you are witness to
Do you feel it?
In the soft skin and fur of your loved ones
Do you sense it?
In the hum of the atoms and the harmony of nature
Do you appreciate it?
In each breath that anchors your light to matter
Do you share it?
In the many unique qualities you have accrued through
experience
Do you believe it as your truth?
Do you embrace it as a virtue?
Do you own it as your center?
Do you define it in your presence?

Do you recognize it every moment?
Do you perceive its depth?
Conceive it as a concept?
Hold a place for it in this world?
Cherish it beyond all reason?
Perpetually channel it forth?
Mimic and personify it?
To know yourself and all through it?
Yes!

How to Transcend

Be aware of your own actions
Experience your own worth
Accept the rejection
At the moment of your birth
Stand by your convictions
Whatever they may bring
Delve into all your talents
To Dance, Act, Write, or Sing
Marvel at the wonders
A Banquet to mankind
Connect with others deep within
Way beyond the mind
Live past the constrictions
Of what one can endure

Raise the bar on accountability

With motives that are pure

Rake the shoals of society

To glean a spark in man

Ignite a billowing fire

As only pure love can

Lift humanity on your shoulders

Let it see that which you see

Beyond the walls of the self

Everyone empowered, inspired and free.

1/25/15

One Thought of You

I indulged in one quick thought of you
Etched it in my mind
It transported me to a world
That alone I could not find

Where Love is not sectioned off in pairs
Single file, one to one
But is lavished generously and prevalent
On every single one

Sincerity is commonplace
Intimacy too
Kind intentions are transparent
In everything we do

Love is not locked away
Allotted to just one heart
It is what all eat, sleep, dream and wear
And which we're all a part

It's not cast off with ill regard
Or based upon a whim
No, love is what we walk through
Dance and fly and swim

One thought of you takes me there
Heals my weary heart
That runs this body in this world of illusion
Where we are all separated and apart

Allow me one quick thought
That transforms me to a place
Where everyone is betrothed to love
In sanctity and grace

I can withstand loneliness
As a temporary state
Love is not a random act
Payment, door prize or fate

Love is not contingent
On believing, hope or prayer
Love is allotted to everyone
Even if no one says, "They care"

Meet me in a land
Devoid of guilt or blame
Where I am allowed to love you
With not one hint of shame

Meet me at the altar
Where in this world is only meant for two
But in this altered Universe
Is shared with everyone and you

I devote my time on earth
To showing others this world too
The one I so easily access
With just one thought of you

2/15/16

Getting to the Heart of It

I am the Muslim, I am the Jew

I am the old lady who lives in the shoe

I am the matador, I am his cape

The targeted bull, at the back of his nape

I am the frenzy, I am the calm

I am the corruption, I am its balm

I am the eagle's discerning keen eye

I am the lawyer and his quick witted lie

I am anywhere, push comes to shove

I am below as I am above

I am every vantage point that helps one to grow

I am the heat wave, I am the snow

Anything that the human heart can endure

I am the infection, I am the cure

I am every experience one needs to surmount

You can knock someone down but don't count them out

You can take their pride and cause them to fall

You can shrivel them up in an energetic ball

But soon we'll all awaken from this illusion and see

That we're all joyful, whole, abundant, loving and free.

1/19/15

About the Author

Jen Ward is an Ascended Master. This entails being a Reiki Master, gifted healer, inspirational speaker, author of many books and an innovator of a healing modality for self empowerment. She offers a simple but dynamic protocol to assist individuals in clearing up all their energy imbalances (karma) with every person, experience, belief system and the Universe. She enables all those struggling, to cross the bridge of self-discovery, with her encouragement and instruction. Her passion is to empower the world by encouraging all individuals in their own miraculous healing adventure.

Jen is considered a Sangoma, a traditional African shaman who channels ancestors, and clears energy by emoting sounds and vocalizations. An interesting prerequisite to being a Sangoma is to have survived being on the brink of death. When it was first revealed that Jen was a Sangoma, she had not yet fulfilled the rigorous prerequisites necessary. However, in April 2008, through a series of traumas, she returned to civilization meeting all the requirements. She passed through the transforming process of enlightenment. She returned to the world of humanity a devout soul inspired to serve.

Jen currently works diligently in the physical world and in the worlds of energy to assist all souls to reach greater heights of awareness and empowerment. Those who believe they have "arrived", may be the most entrenched in the mental realms. They can painlessly free themselves without relinquishing the comfort of their current belief system. All that needs to be released will fall away naturally. "Fear, in all its subtle forms of denial and judgment, will naturally fall away."

Many people report receiving healing assistance from Jen or protection in the dream state and even more subtle realms. Jen is passionate to shatter the mentality of sitting at the feet of another. She shares truth and wisdom graciously and abundantly. Jen makes the practice of doling out truth in increments to set up the dynamic of personality worship obsolete. Her passion is to assist the world over the brink of all perceived limitations, beyond the mind's scope, into the realms of enlightenment.

Other Books by Jen Ward

Enlightenment Unveiled: *Expound into Empowerment.* This book contains case studies to help you peel away the layers to your own empowerment using the tapping technique.

Grow Where You Are Planted: *Quotes for an Enlightened "Jeneration."* Inspirational quotes that are seeds to shift your consciousness into greater awareness.

Perpetual Calendar: *Daily Exercises to Maintain Balance and Harmony in Your Health, Relationships and the Entire World.* 369 days of powerful taps to use as a daily grounding practice for those who find meditation difficult.

Letters of Accord: *Assigning Words to Unspoken Truth.* Truths that the ancient ones want you to know to redirect your life and humanity back into empowerment.

The Do What You Love Diet: *Finally, Finally, Finally, Feel Good in Your Own Skin.* Revolutionary approach to regaining fitness by tackling primal imbalances in relationship to food.

Emerging from the Mist: *Awakening the Balance of Female Empowerment in the World.* Release all the issues that prevent someone from embracing their female empowerment.

Affinity for All Life: *Valuing Your Relationship with all Species.* This book is a means to strengthen and affirm your relationship with the animal kingdom.

The Wisdom of the Trees. If one is struggling for purpose, they can find love, and truth by tuning into the *Wisdom of the Trees.*

Chronicles of Truth. Truth has been buried away for way too long. Here is a means to discover the truth that lies dormant within yourself.

Healing Your Relationships. This book is a means to open up communications and responsiveness to others so that clarity and respect can flourish again in society.

How to Awaken Your Inner Dragon: *Visualizations to Empower Yourself and the World.* Tap into the best possible version of you and the world.

Collecting Everyday Miracles: *Commit to Being Empowered.* This book is a thought provoking means to recreate the moment of conception with everyday miracles. It is through gratitude and awareness. This is what this book fosters.

The SFT Lexicon: *Spiritual Freedom Technique.* Tap into the powerful ability of the mind to self heal.

Past Lives, Dreams and Inspiration. People are starving for truth. Unfortunately, they have been conditioned to dismiss their dreams and all remnants of past lives in discovering their own trajectory connection to truth. This book gives life to the expansiveness of self-discovery through one's past lives and dream experiences. There is no greater form of inspiration than discovering one's own depth.

2018 A Turning Point: *Shift from Primal Mode to Enlightenment.* If in 2018 you sensed a shift in the world, if you sensed an internal struggle happening on the world's behalf, if you are fascinated with truths that are hidden from the masses, or if you have some programming left that you would like to eliminate, this book is for you.

God: *The Ultimate Search Engine.* Finally a book to address all the layers of shame piled on the individual in the name of a vengeful, petty God. Man has spoken for God long enough. It's time to speak to God directly.

All books available on Jen's website, JenuineHealing.com

Made in the USA
Columbia, SC
01 September 2021